The Seven Stages
an
The Insight K

The Seven Stages of Purification and The Insight Knowledges

The Venerable Mahāthera
Matara Sri Ñāṇārāma

Translated from the Sinhala

Buddhist Publication Society
Kandy • Sri Lanka

Buddhist Publication Society
P.O. Box 61
54, Sangharaja Mawatha
Kandy, Sri Lanka

First published 1983
Second edition 1993
Reprinted 2000

National Library of Sri Lanka –
Cataloguing–in–Publication Data

Sri Ñāṇārāma himi, Matara

The Seven Stages of Purification and The Insight Knowledges: a guide to the progressive stages of Buddhist meditation: Matara Sri Ñāṇārāma himi – 3rd impression – Kandy : Buddhist Publication Society, 2000
80p.; 22cm– First published in 1983

ISBN 955–24–0059–7

i. 294.34435 DDC 21 ii. Title
1. Meditation (Buddhism) 2. Buddhism

ISBN 955-24-0059-7

Typeset at the BPS

Printed in Sri Lanka
M.D. Gunasena & Co. (Printers) Ltd.,
20 St. Sebastian Hill
Colombo 12

CONTENTS

Preface vii
List of Abbreviations ix

Introduction: The Relay of Chariots 1

I. Purification of Virtue 5

II. Purification of Mind 8

1. The Obstructions and Aids to Concentration 8
2. The Stages of Concentration 15

III. Purification of View 19

IV. Purification by Overcoming Doubt 23

V. Purification by Knowledge and Vision of What is Path and Not-Path 29

1. Knowledge by Comprehension 30
2. The Ten Imperfections of Insight 35
3. The Path and the Not-Path 39

VI. Purification by Knowledge and Vision of the Way 40

1. The Three Full Understandings 40
2. The Progress of Insight Knowledge 41

(1) Knowledge of Contemplation of Arising and Passing Away 42
(*Udayabbayānupassanāñāṇa*)

(2) Knowledge of Contemplation of Dissolution 47
(*Bhangānupassanāñāṇa*)

(3) Knowledge of Appearance as Terror 47
(*Bhay'upaṭṭhānañāṇa*)

(4) Knowledge of Contemplation of Danger 48
(*Ādīnavānupassanāñāṇa*)

(5) Knowledge of Contemplation of Disenchantment 48
(*Nibbidānupassanāñāṇa*)

(6) Knowledge of Desire for Deliverance 49
(*Muñcitukamyatāñāṇa*)

(7) Knowledge of Contemplation of Reflection 50
(*Paṭisankhānupassanāñāṇa*)

(8) Knowledge of Equanimity about Formations 51
(*Saṅkhār'upekkhāñāṇa*)

(9) Knowledge in Conformity with Truth or Conformity Knowledge 53
(*Anulomañāṇa*)

VII. Purification by Knowledge and Vision 54

1. Insight Leading to Emergence 54
2. Change-of-lineage Knowledge 57
3. The Supramundane Paths and Fruits 59
4. Reviewing Knowledge 62

Conclusion 63

Appendices

1. The Call to the Meditative Life 65
2. The Eighteen Principal Insights 68
3. The Cognitive Series in Jhāna and the Path 70
4. Oneness 73

About the Author 75

TRANSLATOR'S PREFACE

If the output of literature on a subject is any indication of the prevailing trends in the reading public, Buddhist meditation is today undoubtedly a subject of wide interest both in the East and in the West. In this field, the West is beginning to look to the venerable traditions of the East to learn more of the techniques and teachings of mind-control. The "supply"of this "know-how" for self-conquest, however, falls far short of the "demand" due to the dearth of meditation masters who can speak with confidence on the subject. It is in this context that the present treatise should prove to be a mine of information for those who cherish higher ideals.

The author of this treatise is our revered teacher, the Venerable Matara Sri Ñāṇārāma Mahāthera—the meditation master (*kammaṭṭhānācariya*) of Mitirigala Nissaraṇa Vanaya, at Mitirigala, Sri Lanka. Now in his eightieth year, he is one of the most respected among the meditation masters of Sri Lanka today, both for his all-round knowledge of the techniques of meditation and for his long experience in guiding disciples. Although he himself specialized in the Burmese *vipassanā* methods and is able to speak with authority on the subject, he does not confine himself to the "pure insight" approach. Though presented succinctly, his treatise covers the entire range of the Seven Stages of Purification and the Insight Knowledges, stressing the value of both *samatha* (serenity) and *vipassanā* (insight).

The treatise grew out of a series of discourses on meditation which our venerable teacher gave to us, his pupils, in 1977. Some of us managed to take down the substance of his talks, which we later put to him and elaborated on with some editorial comments. The final result of these labours appeared as the original Sinhala treatise which bore the title *Sapta Visuddhiya-ha-Vidarshana-ñāṇa*. The Sinhala work was then translated into an exact English version, which was further polished and edited until it took shape as the present treatise.

In transforming the spoken discourses into a systematic exposition, to some extent the living spirit of their immediate delivery had to be lost. We have tried to prevent this loss by retaining as many of the inspirational passages as we could in the body of the text. A few such passages from the early talks had to be removed as being out of place in an expository treatise. But to make these available to the reader, we include them in Appendix 1 under the title: " The Call to the Meditative Life."

A Pupil

Mitirigala Nissaraṇa Vanaya
Mitirigala,
Sri Lanka

October 25, 1981

LIST OF ABBREVIATIONS

A.	Anguttara Nikāya
D.	Dīgha Nikāya
Dhp.	Dhammapada
Dhp.A.	Dhammapadaṭṭhakathā (Comm.)
G.S.	Gradual Sayings
K.S.	Kindred Sayings
M.	Majjhima Nikāya
MA.	Majjhima Nikāyaṭṭhakathā (*Papañcasūdanī*)
M.L.S.	Middle Length Sayings
Mp.	Milindapañhā
Pj.	Paramatthajotika
Ps.	Paṭisambhidāmagga
S.	Saṁyutta Nikāya
Sn.	Suttanipāta
Thag.	Theragāthā
Ud.	Udāna
Vism.	Visuddhimagga

References to the *Visuddhimagga* are to chapter and section number of the translation by Bhikkhu Ñāṇamoli, *The Path of Purification,* 4th ed. (BPS, 1979).

Namo tassa bhagavato arahato sammāsambuddhassa

Homage be to the Blessed One, Accomplished and
Fully Enlightened

INTRODUCTION

The Relay of Chariots

The path of practice leading to the attainment of Nibbāna unfolds in seven stages, known as the Seven Stages of Purification (*satta visuddhi*). The seven in order are:

1. Purification of Virtue (*sīlavisuddhi*)
2. Purification of Mind (*cittavisuddhi*)
3. Purification of View (*diṭṭhivisuddhi*)
4. Purification by Overcoming Doubt (*kankhāvitaraṇavisuddhi*)
5. Purification by Knowledge and Vision of What is Path and Not-Path (*maggāmaggañāṇadassanavisuddhi*)
6. Purification by Knowledge and Vision of the Way (*paṭipadāñāṇadassanavisuddhi*)
7. Purification by Knowledge and Vision (*ñāṇadassanavisuddhi*).

In the attainment of Nibbāna itself, our minds are in direct relation to the seventh and last stage of this series, the Purification by Knowledge and Vision, which is the knowledge of the supramundane path. But this purification cannot be attained all at once, since the seven stages of purification form a causally related series in which one has to pass through the first six purifications before one can arrive at the seventh.

The only direct canonical reference to the Seven Stages of Purification is found in the Rathavinīta Sutta (The Discourse on the Relay of Chariots), the twenty-fourth discourse of the Majjhima Nikāya.[1] In the Dasuttara Sutta of the Dīgha Nikāya (Sutta No. 34), these seven purifications are counted among nine items collectively called factors of endeavour tending to purification (*pāri-*

1. Translated by I.B. Horner as *Middle Length Sayings* (M.L.S.), 3 volumes (London: Pali Text Society, 1954-59).

suddhi-padhāniyanga), the last two of which are purification of wisdom and purification of deliverance. However, this same series of seven purifications forms the scaffolding of Bhadantācariya Buddhaghosa's encyclopedic manual of Buddhist meditation, the *Visuddhimagga*. Thus this series serves as a most succinct outline of the entire path a meditator passes through in his inner journey from bondage to liberation.

In the Rathavinita Sutta, the Seven Stages of Purification are presented through a dialogue in which the questions of the venerable Sāriputta are met with striking replies from the venerable Puṇṇa Mantāṇiputta—all meant to highlight some salient features of this teaching:

> "Friend, is the holy life lived under the Blessed One?"
> "Yes, friend."
> "Friend, is it for purification of virtue that the holy life is lived under the Blessed One?"
> "Not for this, friend."
> "Then, friend, is it for purification of mind that the holy life is lived under the Blessed One?"
> "Not for this, friend."
> "Then friend, is it for purification of view that the holy life is lived under the Blessed One?"
> "Not for this, friend."
> "Then, friend, is it for purification by overcoming doubt that the holy life is lived under the Blessed One?"
> "Not for this, friend."
> "Then, friend, is it for purification by knowledge and vision of what is path and not-path that the holy life is lived under the Blessed One?"
> "Not for this, friend."
> "Then, friend, is it for purification by knowledge and vision of the way that the holy life is lived under the Blessed One?"
> "Not for this, friend."
> "Then, friend, is it for purification by knowledge and vision that the holy life is lived under the Blessed One?"
> "Not for this, friend."
> "What, then, is the purpose, friend, of living the holy life under the Blessed One?"
> "Friend, it is for the complete extinction without grasping that the holy life is lived under the Blessed One."

This reply reveals that not even the seventh and last purification is to be regarded as the purpose of living the holy life. The purpose is nothing but the complete extinction of all defilements without any kind of grasping. In other words, it is the attainment of Nibbāna—the Uncompounded Element (*asankhata dhātu*).

To clarify this point further, the venerable Puṇṇa Mantāṇiputta gives the following parable of the Relay of Chariots:

> "Friend, it is as though while King Pasenadi of Kosala was staying in Sāvatthī, something to be done urgently should arise in Sāketa, and seven relays of chariots would be arranged for him between Sāvatthī and Sāketa. Then, friend, King Pasenadi of Kosala, having left Sāvatthī by the palace-gate, might mount the first chariot in the relay, and by means of the first chariot in the relay, he would reach the second chariot in the relay. He would dismiss the first chariot in the relay and would mount the second chariot in the relay, and by means of the second chariot in the relay, he would reach the third chariot in the relay. He would dismiss the second chariot in the relay and would mount the third chariot in the relay, and by means of the third chariot in the relay, he would reach the fourth chariot in the relay. He would dismiss the third chariot in the relay and would mount the fourth chariot in the relay, and by means of the fourth chariot in the relay, he would reach the fifth chariot in the relay. He would dismiss the fourth chariot in the relay and would mount the fifth chariot in the relay, and by means of the fifth chariot in the relay, he would reach the sixth chariot in the relay. He would dismiss the fifth chariot in the relay and would mount the sixth chariot in the relay, and by means of the sixth chariot in the relay, he would reach the seventh chariot in the relay. He would dismiss the sixth chariot in the relay and would mount the seventh chariot in the relay, and by means of the seventh chariot in the relay, he would reach the palace-gate in Sāketa."

In the case of the seven purifications, the purity implied is reckoned in terms of the elimination of the unwholesome factors opposed to each purification. *Purification of Virtue* implies the purity obtained through abstinence from bodily and verbal misconduct as well as from wrong livelihood. *Purification of Mind* is the purity resulting from cleansing the mind of attachment, aversion, inertia, restlessness and conflict, and from securing it against their influx. *Purification of View* is brought about by dispelling the distortions of wrong views. *Purification by Overcoming Doubt* is purity through the conquest of all doubts concerning the pattern of saṁsāric existence. *Purification by Knowledge and Vision of What is Path and Not-Path* signifies the purity attained by passing beyond the alluring distractions which arise in the course of insight meditation. *Purification by Knowledge and Vision of the Way* is the purity resulting from the temporary removal of defilements which obstruct the path of practice. And lastly, *Purification by Knowledge and Vision* is the complete purity gained by eradicating defilements together with their underlying tendencies by means of the supramundane paths. Purification by Knowledge and Vision consists of the knowledges of the four paths—the path of Stream-entry, the path of Once-return, the path of Non-return and the path of Arahantship.

CHAPTER I

PURIFICATION OF VIRTUE
(*Sīlavisuddhi*)

Like any other tree, the great tree of the meditative life requires roots. The roots of the meditative life are Purification of Virtue and Purification of Mind. Unless these two roots are nourished, there will be no progress in meditation.

The first and most fundamental of the roots is *Purification of Virtue*. Purification of Virtue consists in understanding and maintaining four types of restraint: (1) observing the precepts one has undertaken and protecting them like one's very life; (2) guarding the six sense-doors without allowing defilements to arise; (3) maintaining a righteous livelihood; and (4) making use of one's requisites of life with wise reflection. A meditative monk who lives according to these four ways of restraint will find nothing to get attached to or resent. The meditator, then, is one who has a "light" livelihood, being light in body and content at heart—free from the burden of ownership as regards anything anywhere between the earth and the sky. Though these four principles were originally prescribed for monks and nuns, lay meditators should adapt them to their own situation.

Everyone must have a standard of virtue dedicated to Nibbāna. The standard is relative to his status in life. Monks and nuns are expected to observe the precepts of training given in the two codes of moral discipline making up their respective Pātimokkhas. Male and female novices have to keep the ten precepts as their standard of virtue. Male and female lay-devotees have five precepts as a permanent standard of virtue in their everyday life. If they are more enthusiastic, they can undertake and keep the "eight precepts with livelihood as the eighth," or the ten lay precepts, or the eight precepts recommended as the special observance for Uposatha days. The texts record several instances of persons who, without previously undertaking any precepts, fulfilled the requirements of the Purification of Virtue by a mere act of determination while listening to a discourse, and even succeeded in attaining the supramundane paths and fruits. We should understand that such persons were endowed with highly developed spiritual faculties and were backed by a vast store of merit lying to their credit since they had already fulfilled the perfections for their respective attainments in the past.

At the time of attaining the paths and fruits, both monk and layman should be equally developed in regard to the virtue of sense restraint. This virtue of sense restraint consists in mindfully guarding the six sense-doors—the eye, ear, nose, tongue, body and mind. By means of mindfulness one must prevent the arising of all defilements sparked off by sense experience—all forms of desires, major and minor conflicts, as well as those deceptions which are extremely subtle, rooted in delusion itself, in pure and simple ignorance. Deception is something difficult to understand. But if one mindfully makes a mental note of every object "calling" at the six sense-doors, one can free oneself from deception. The not-knowing and misconceiving of what should be known amounts to delusion.

By failing to make a mental note of a pleasant feeling, one provides an opportunity for lust to arise. Failure to make a mental note of an unpleasant feeling can be an opportunity for the arising of repugnance, while such a failure in regard to a neither-unpleasant-nor-pleasant feeling might give rise to deception, delusion or ignorance. Therefore the practice of mentally noting each and every object that calls at the six sense-doors will also be helpful in getting rid of the underlying tendency to ignorance.

> In the case of the pleasant feeling, friend Visākha, the underlying tendency to attachment must be abandoned. In the case of the painful feeling, the underlying tendency to repugnance must be abandoned. And in the case of the neither-unpleasant-nor-pleasant feeling, the underlying tendency to ignorance must be abandoned.
>
> Cūlavedalla Sutta, M.I,303

Before one can establish oneself firmly in virtue, one must understand its significance well. For this purpose, one should study the Description of Virtue in the *Visuddhimagga* (Chapter I).

Normally, one protects one's virtue impelled by conscience and shame (*hiri, ottappa*), which are its proximate causes. A wise man, however, observes virtue purely with the aim of attaining

Nibbāna. As a matter of fact, virtue has been defined as the bodily and verbal restraint (the abstention from bodily and verbal misconduct) which comes as a result of listening to and understanding the Dhamma (Ps.I,1).

There are several grades of virtue, ranked in order of ascending excellence:

1. the virtue of an ordinary worlding (i.e. one who is not practising to attain the supramundane path);
2. the virtue of a noble worldling (i.e. a worldling practising the course of training to reach the path);
3. the virtue of a trainer (i.e. the virtue associated with the four paths and the first three fruits);
4. the virtue of a non-trainer (i.e. the virtue consisting in tranquillized purification or virtue associated with the fruit of Arahantship).

The fourth and last of these is the virtue which comes naturally to Buddhas, Paccekabuddhas and Arahants as a result of their eradication of all defilements.

Understanding the virtue of fourfold restraint described above, one should protect one's virtue even at the cost of life, being guided by conscience and shame as well as by the ideal of Nibbāna.

CHAPTER II

PURIFICATION OF MIND
(*Cittavisuddhi*)

The bodily and verbal restraint established by purified virtue paves the way for mental restraint, which brings the next stage of purification, *Purification of Mind.* This purification comes through concentration (*samādhi*), which can be reached by two approaches, the vehicle of serenity (*samathayāna*) or the vehicle of insight (*vipassanāyāna*).

1. The Obstructions and Aids to Concentration

A meditator intent on developing serenity concentration must first make an effort to sever the impediments to meditation. For meditative monks, the *Visuddhimagga* enumerates ten impediments (*palibodhā*):

> A dwelling, family and gain,
> A class, and building too, as fifth
> And travel, kin, affliction, books,
> And supernormal powers: ten.[1]

1. A *dwelling* can be an impediment to one who has many belongings stored there or whose mind is caught up by some business connected with it.

2. A *family* consisting of relatives or supporters becomes an impediment for one living in close association with its members.

3. *Gains*, in the sense of the four requisites of a monk's life (robes, food, lodgings and medicines), oblige him to become involved in association with laymen.

4. A *class* of students is an impediment when it binds the meditator with duties of teaching and instruction.

5. New *building work* is always an impediment to a meditating monk as it is a responsibility which distracts him.

1. See Vism. III, 29-56.

6. A *journey* becomes a source of distracting thoughts both in the planning and in the actual travel.

7. *Kin* or relatives, when they fall sick, sometimes have to be cared for by a monk, a responsibility which again takes him away from meditation.

8. One's own illness or *affliction* which calls for treatment is yet another impediment.

9. *Books*, in the sense of responsibility for the scriptures, can be a hindrance to some meditators.

10. Even the *supernormal powers*, which are hard to maintain, may be an impediment for one who seeks insight.

It will be useful to a meditating monk to understand beforehand the way of tackling the impediments.[2] Six impediments—dwelling, family, gain, class, kin and fame— can be overcome by giving up attachment to them. Three impediments—building, travel and books—are done away with by not undertaking the activities they imply. Affliction is an impediment to be overcome by proper medical treatment with regard to curable diseases. There are some diseases which are of the chronic type. However, whether one's disease turns out to be chronic or even incurable, one should go on meditating in spite of it. Diseases like catarrh, which are rather tolerable, must be subdued with perseverance in meditation. An earnest meditator must not allow illness to get the better of him. In countless births in *saṁsāra* one must have been the helpless victim of diseases. So at least now one should make a sincere effort to treat the diseases of the mind even while taking medicines for the diseases of the body. In this way one will succeed in overcoming the impediments so that one can go on with one's meditation.

Besides knowing how to cut off the impediments, a meditator should understand the six obstacles (*paripantha*) and the six cleansings (*vodāna*). The obstacles are those conditions which mar or retard progress in concentration, the cleansings those which help bring concentration to maturity. The six obstacles are:

1. the mind hankering after the past, overcome by distraction;
2. the mind yearning for the future, overcome by hopes and longings;

---

2. A lay-meditator will, of course, not be able to avoid the impediments as fully as a monk, but he should try to emulate the monk to the best of his ability (Ed.).

3. the inert mind, overcome by lethargy;
4. the over-anxious mind, overcome by restlessness;
5. the over-inclined mind, overcome by lust;
6. the disinclined mind, overcome by ill will. (Ps.I,165)

Understanding that these six conditions are detrimental to concentration, one should constantly protect the mind from falling under their influence, for through carelessness, one can lose whatever concentration one has already developed.

Now, let us see how these six states occur. When the meditator applies himself to his subject of meditation, thoughts relating to that subject keep on arising in his mind. And as this train of thought continues to run along the track of the meditation subject, now and then it runs into memories of certain *past events* in some way related to that subject. Before the meditator is aware of what is happening, the train of thought jumps off the track of meditation and adheres to those past events. It may take some time, even a long time, for the meditator to realize that his mind is no longer on the meditation subject. This tendency for the mind to deviate from the meditation subject greatly impairs the power of concentration, causing distraction. Thus this tendency is a hindrance even to the maintenance of one's concentration, let alone its maturing.

The *second obstacle* cited above is the tendency of the mind to run toward the future. Very often this tendency takes the form of wishes and aspirations. When desire takes hold of the mind for a long while, it creates a certain mental tremor, and this too undermines concentration.

The *third obstacle* is mental inertia, which makes the mind lethargic.

The *fourth obstacle* is the over-anxious mind. At times the meditator becomes so enthusiastic and strenuous in his efforts that he begins to meditate with excessive zeal. But neither his body nor his mind can stand this overstrung effort. Physically he feels exhausted and sometimes has headaches; mentally he becomes very confused, leading to the decline of his concentration.

The *fifth obstacle* is the over-inclined state of mind. This state is brought about by lust and results from allowing the mind to stray among various extraneous thought-objects.

And the *sixth obstacle* is the disinclined state of the mind which results from allowing the mind to pursue extraneous thought-objects under the influence of ill will.

To protect the mind from lapsing into these six obstacles, one should prevent the mind from pursuing extraneous thought-objects. It is by keeping one's mind aloof from these six obstacles that the six occasions for the cleansing of concentration are obtained. In other words, in the very attempt to overcome the six obstacles, one fulfils the six conditions necessary for the cleansing of concentration. The six cleansings are thus the cleansing of the mind from hankering after the past, from yearning for the future, from lethargy, from restlessness, from lust and from ill will.

A certain degree of purification of the mind is brought about by these six ways of cleansing concentration. However, four more auxiliary conditions are necessary to complete this purification:

1. The two spiritual faculties, faith and wisdom, must be kept in balance.
2. All five spiritual faculties (faith, energy, mindfulness, concentration and wisdom) must function with a unity of purpose.
3. The right amount of effort must be applied.
4. Constant and repeated practice must be maintained.

Ps.I,168

Faith, in this context, means the absence of doubts in regard to one's subject of meditation. It is confidence in one's ability to succeed in practice. Wisdom implies the understanding of the purpose of one's meditation. The purpose should be the arousing of the knowledge of mind-and-matter (*nāma-rūpa*). The "right amount of effort" is moderate effort. Generally, in the case of serenity meditation (e.g. mindfulness of breathing), three sittings of three hours duration each would be sufficient practice for a day, whereas in insight meditation, one has to go on meditating in all postures throughout the day. By "repeated practice" is meant the arousing of a special ability or a specific tendency by repeatedly dwelling on some wholesome thought.

To develop concentration, all one's actions—large or small—must be done with mindfulness. One should make a special resolve to do everything with the right amount of mindfulness. When each and every act of a meditator is done mindfully, all his actions will begin to maintain a certain level of uniformity. And as this uniformity in mindfulness develops, the behaviour of the meditator's mind will also reach a certain level of progress. Owing to this power, all postures of a meditator will be uniformly smooth and even. His deportment, the inner wealth of his virtues, will be of an inspiring nature.

At the outset, the task of developing mindfulness and concentration might appear as something difficult or even unnecessary. One might even become discouraged by it. Understanding this possibility beforehand, one should make a firm determination to persist in one's practice. The progress of a meditator is nothing other than his progress in mindfulness and concentration. When, at the very start, one enthusiastically sets about developing mindfulness, when one makes an earnest effort to apply mindfulness, one will begin to see how the mind becomes receptive to mindfulness—almost unwittingly. And once one becomes used to it, one will be able to practise mindfulness without any difficulty. One will then come to feel that mindfulness is an activity quite in harmony with the nature of the mind. And ultimately, the meditator can reach a level at which he can practise mindfulness effortlessly. Not only that, but he will also discover how mindfulness, when developed, overflows into concentration. As mindfulness develops, concentration naturally develops along with it. But an unbroken effort is necessary, and if one is to maintain unbroken mindfulness, one must pay attention to the intervals which occur at the change of postures.

There are four postures: sitting, standing, walking and lying down. In sitting meditation, the mind becomes calm. But when the meditators rise up from their seats, some lose that calmness. Their mindfulness and concentration disappear. Having gotten up, when they start walking or pacing up and down, they lose even the little calmness they had when standing. Their mindfulness and concentration dissipate still more. Because of this tardy procedure, this lack of unbroken continuous mindfulness, one goes on meditating every day, but makes no worthwhile progress; one stagnates.

If one is to avoid this serious drawback, *one should direct one's attention to every posture-junction*. Take, for example, the walking posture. This is a posture which offers an excellent opportunity to arouse the power of concentration. Many meditators find it easy to develop concentration in this posture. Suppose one has aroused some degree of mindfulness and concentration while walking. Now, when one intends to sit down, one should see to it that one does not lose what one has already gained. With concentration, one should make a mental note of the intention of sitting: 'intending to sit, intending to sit.' Then, in sitting down also, make a mental note: 'sitting, sitting.' In this manner one should maintain unbroken whatever mindfulness and concentration one has already built up, and continue one's meditation in the sitting posture. This practice of making a mental note of both the intention and the act at the posture-junctions enables one to maintain mindfulness and concentration without any lapses.

In trying to maintain unbroken mindfulness, one should consider well the dangers of neglecting that practice and the benefits of developing it. To develop mindfulness is to develop heedfulness, which is helpful to all wholesome mental states. To neglect mindfulness is to grow in heedlessness, the path leading to all unwholesome states, to downfall. With these considerations, one should make a firm determination and really try to develop mindfulness. When mindfulness develops, concentration, too, develops. Note that it is the development of mindfulness and concentration that is called "progress in meditation." Always bear in mind the Buddha's words:

> He who has mindfulness is always well;
> The mindful one grows in happiness. (S.I, 208)

A meditator has to pay attention to the application of mindfulness at all times and under all circumstances. What needs special emphasis here is that the application of mindfulness should be so oriented as to lead one onward to the realization of Nibbāna. Mindfulness has to be taken up in a way and in a spirit that will effectively arouse the knowledge of the supramundane paths. It is only then that mindfulness can rightfully be called "the enlightenment-factor of mindfulness" (*satisambojjhanga*). Such mindfulness, well attuned to the path, leads to the goal of Nibbāna.

Meditation is a battle with the mind. It is a battle with the enemies within—the mental defilements. First of all, one has to recognize that these enemies, while battling among themselves, are at war with the good thoughts, too. "Love" is fighting with "anger." "Jealousy" is in complicity with "anger." "Greed" steps in as an ally to "conceit" and "views." "Views" and "conceit" are mutually opposed, though they both owe their origin to "greed."

The meditator should understand the nature of these defilements. Mental defilements are a gang of crafty enemies. They create deceptions in the meditator's mind even when meditation shows signs of progress. The meditator becomes happy. But this is a case of subtle deception. Because of his complacency, meditation tends to decline. This is an instance of an enemy masquerading as a friend.

Self-deceptions can occur even when the meditator is engaged in making a mental note. For instance, in mentally noting a painful feeling, if he has the intention of putting an end to that pain, hate will find an opportunity to step in. Similarly, in mentally noting a desirable object, the meditator is rather tardy in doing so. This lapse leaves room for greed to creep in. In fact, he deliberately delays the mental noting in order to give an opportunity to his desire. He does this when the object of which he has a mental image happens to be a pleasant one. Sometimes, in such situations, he totally neglects the mental noting. The loss the meditator incurs by this neglect is indescribably great.

Failure to make a mental note of an object as such becomes a serious drawback in the development of one's meditative attention. As soon as one sees a pleasant object, one should make a mental note of it and summarily dismiss it. Otherwise one will only be courting disaster. Sometimes the meditator will get a mental image of a woman coming so close as to make physical contact with him. On such occasions the meditator has to be alert and heedful in making a mental note. There are two ways of mental noting:

(1) While meditating, one hears a sound. If it is a sound which continues for a long while, one should mentally note it twice or thrice ('hearing'...'hearing').

(2) While meditating, one hears a sound. If it is possible to continue meditation in spite of that sound, after the initial mental noting, one need not repeatedly make a mental note of it.

In meditation, one should make a mental note of everything encountered. One should get into the habit of mentally noting whatever comes along—be it big or small, good or bad. To make a mental note of painful feelings with dislike leaves room for hate, thus one should always exercise equanimity in mentally noting these feelings. One should not note them with the idea of getting rid of them. The aim should be to comprehend the nature of phenomena by understanding pain as pain. The same principle applies to a pleasant object giving rise to a pleasant feeling. With Nibbāna as the sole aim, one should learn to make mental notes of everything with equanimity.

2. The Stages of Concentration

Purification of Mind is achieved when the degree of concentration becomes sufficiently strong to cause the suppression of the five afflictive defilements known as the "five hindrances" (*pañcanīvaraṇā*), namely: sensual desire, ill will, sloth and torpor, agitation and remorse, and doubt.[3]

There are three kinds of concentration qualifying as Purification of Mind: access concentration (*upacāra-samādhi*), absorption concentration (*appanā-samādhi*), and momentary concentration (*khaṇika-samādhi*). The first two are achieved through the vehicle of serenity (*samatha*), the last through the vehicle of insight (*vipassanā*). Momentary concentration possesses the same strength of mental unification as access concentration. Since it is equipped with the ten conditions mentioned above, and holds the five hindrances at bay, it aids the attainment of insight knowledge. However, because it does not serve directly as a basis for jhāna as such, it is not called access concentration.

Here we will discuss the attainment of Purification of Mind via the approach of serenity. The fullest form of this purification is absorption concentration, which consists of eight meditative attainments (*aṭṭha samāpatti*): four absorptions called *jhānas*, and four immaterial states (*āruppas*). The two main preparatory stages leading up to a jhāna are called preliminary work (*parikamma*) and access (*upacāra*).[4]

The ordinary consciousness cannot be converted into an exalted level all at once, but has to be transformed by degrees. In the stage of preliminary work, one must go on attending to the subject of meditation for a long time until the spiritual faculties become balanced and function with a unity of purpose. Once the spiritual faculties gain that balance, the mind drops into access. In the access stage, the five hindrances do not disrupt the flow of concentration. The original gross object of meditation is replaced by a subtle mental image called the counterpart sign (*paṭibhāga-nimitta*).

During the access stage, the mind becomes powerfully unified

3. (1) *kāmacchanda*, (2) *vyāpāda*, (3) *thinamiddha*, (4) *uddhaccakukkucca*, (5) *vicikicchā*.

4. See Appendix 3 for further details.

upon its object. When the mind, as it were, sinks into the object, this signals the arising of the jhānic mind known as absorption. On reviewing the first jhāna, one discovers that it has five distinguishing components called "jhāna factors," namely: applied thought, sustained thought, joy, bliss and one-pointedness.[5]

However, one should not set about the task of reviewing these jhāna factors as soon as one attains a jhāna. To start with, it is advisable to emerge from the jhāna after remaining in it for just five minutes. Even this has to be done with an appropriate determination: "I will attain to the first jhāna for five minutes and emerge from it after five minutes." Using such a formal determination, one should repeat emerging from the jhāna and re-attaining it a good many times. This kind of practice is necessary because there is a danger that a beginner who remains immersed in a jhāna too long will develop excessive attachment to it. This elementary practice is, at the same time, a useful training for mastery in attaining to and emerging from a jhāna.[6]

To prevent any possible distractions and to stabilise the jhāna he has obtained, the beginner should spend his time attaining to and emerging from the jhāna as many times as he can. But on each occasion he should make a fresh determination as to the duration of the jhāna. The number of minutes may be increased gradually. As to the number of times, there need not be any limit. The purpose of this practice is to gain the twin mastery in attaining to and emerging from the jhāna. Mastery in these two respects can be regarded as complete when one is able to remain in the jhāna for exactly the same number of minutes as determined, and is able to emerge from the jhāna at the predetermined time.

Once this twofold mastery is complete, one should practise for mastery in adverting and reviewing. Of these, the practice of adverting should be taken up first as this enables one to consider the jhāna factors separately. Then one can practise for mastery in reviewing, which is a kind of reflection on the quality of those jhāna factors. As it is impossible to reflect on the jhāna factors while remaining in the jhāna, one has to do so only after emerging from it. At the stage of the first jhāna the principal components are the five mental factors: applied thought, sustained thought, joy, bliss and one-pointedness. If these factors are not

5. (1) *vitakka*, (2) *vicāra*, (3) *pīti*, (4)*sukha*, (5) *ekaggatā* .

6. The five kinds of mastery: (1) mastery in adverting, (2) mastery in attaining, (3) mastery in resolving, (4) mastery in emerging, (5) mastery in reviewing.

clearly distinguishable, the meditator should repeatedly attain to and emerge from the jhāna, reviewing it again and again.

"Applied thought" (*vitakka*) is the application of the mind to the object, the "thrusting" of the mind into the object. "Sustained thought" (*vicāra*) is the continued working of the mind on that same object. The distinction between these two will be clearly discernible at this stage because of the purity of the jhānic mind. The other three factors, joy, bliss and one-pointedness, will appear even more distinctively before the mind's eye.

It will be necessary to apply one's mind to these three factors a number of times in direct and reverse order so as to examine their quality. It is in this way that one fulfils the requirements of mastery in adverting and reviewing. In the process of examining the jhāna factors in direct and reverse order, one acquires further mastery in attaining to and emerging from the jhāna.

While examining the jhāna factors in this way to acquire mastery in adverting and reviewing, some of the factors will begin to appear as gross because they have a tendency towards the hindrances. Then one comes to feel that one would be better off without these gross factors. At this juncture one should make the following determination for the attainment of the second jhāna: "May I attain the second jhāna which is free from the two factors of applied thought and sustained thought and which consists of the three factors—joy, bliss and one-pointedness."[7]

After making this determination, the meditator again concentrates his mind on the counterpart sign. When his faculties mature, he passes through all the antecedent stages and enters absorption in the second jhāna, which is free from applied thought and sustained thought, and is endowed with purified joy, bliss and one-pointedness. As in the case of the first jhāna, here too he has to practise for the fivefold mastery, but this time the work is easier and quicker.

---

7. Here in our explanation, we follow the system of the suttas. But to some meditators, only applied thought appears as gross, while to others, both applied thought and sustained thought appear at once as gross. This difference in judgement is due to previous experiences in meditation in past births. The distinction between the fourfold reckoning of the jhānas in the suttas and the fivefold reckoning in the Abhidhamma is a recognition of this difference. "So that which is the second in the fourfold reckoning becomes the second and third in the fivefold reckoning by being divided into two. And those which are the third and fourth in the former reckoning become the fourth and fifth in this reckoning. The first remains the first in each case" (Vism. IV, 202).

After mastering the second jhāna, the meditator may want to go further along the path of serenity. He sees that the joy (*pîti*) of the second jhāna is gross, and that above this there is a third jhāna which has bliss and one-pointedness only. He makes the determination, undertakes the practice, and—if he is capable—attains it. After mastering this jhāna in the five ways, he realizes that bliss is gross, and aspires to reach the fourth jhāna, where blissful feeling is replaced by equanimous feeling, which is more peaceful and sublime. When his practice matures, he enters this jhāna, perfects it, and reviews it.

Beyond the fourth jhāna lie four higher attainments, called "immaterial states"or "immaterial jhānas," since even the subtle material form of the jhānas is absent. These states are named: the base of infinite space, the base of infinite consciousness, the base of nothingness, and the base of neither-perception-nor-non-perception.[8] They are attained by perfecting the power of concentration, not through refining the mental factors, but through training the mind to apprehend increasingly more subtle objects of attention.

---

8. In Pali: (1) *ākāsānañcāyatana*, (2) *viññāṇañcāyatana*, (3) *ākiñcaññāyatana*, (4) *n'eva saññānāsaññāyatana*.

CHAPTER III

PURIFICATION OF VIEW
(*Diṭṭhivisuddhi*)

Purification of Mind is achieved by eliminating the five hindrances through the development of concentration. This can be done through either the vehicle of serenity or the vehicle of insight. The meditator in the vehicle of serenity aims at gaining either access concentration or absorption concentration pertaining to one of the eight levels of attainment—the four jhānas and the four immaterial states. The vehicle of insight aims at gaining momentary concentration by contemplating changing phenomena with mindfulness. When Purification of Mind is accomplished and the mind has become concentrated, the meditator is prepared for insight meditation in order to develop wisdom.

The first stage of insight meditation is called Purification of View. This purification consists in arousing insight into mind-and-matter (*nāmarūpa*), using the meditation subject as a basis. Here the aspect "matter" (*rūpa*) covers the physical side of existence, the aggregate of material form. The aspect "mind" (*nāma*) covers the mental side of existence, the four mental aggregates of feeling, perception, mental formations and consciousness. Purification of View is attained as the meditator goes on attending to his meditation subject with a unified mind equipped with the six cleansings and the four conditions relating to the development of the spiritual faculties. (See pp. 9–11.)

Now the meditation subject begins to appear to him as consisting of two functionally distinguishable parts—mind and matter—rather than as a single unit. This purification gains its name because it marks the initial breakaway from all speculative views headed by personality view.[1] The method employed is a sequence

1. *Sakkāyadiṭṭhi.* The false personality view is the view of a truly existent self related to the five aggregates. It takes on twenty forms according to whether any of the aggregates—form, feeling, perception, mental formations and consciousness—is regarded as identical with self, as belonging to the self, as contained in the self, or as enclosing the self.

of realizations called "abandoning by substitution of opposites" (*tadangappahāna*). The abandoning by substitution of opposites is the abandoning of any given state that ought to be abandoned by means of a particular factor of knowledge, which, as a constituent of insight, is opposed to it. It is like the abandoning of darkness at night by means of a light. (See Vism.XXII,112.)

In the development of insight meditation, there are *sixteen kinds of knowledge* to be obtained in sequence:

1. Knowledge of Delimitation of Mind-and-Matter (*nāmarūpaparicchedañāṇa*)
2. Knowledge of Discerning Cause and Condition (*paccayapariggahañāṇa*)
3. Knowledge of Comprehension (*sammasanañāṇa*)
4. Knowledge of Contemplation of Arising and Passing Away (*udayabbayānupassanāñāṇa*)
5. Knowledge of Contemplation of Dissolution (*bhaṅgānupassanāñāṇa*)
6. Knowledge of Contemplation of Appearance as Terror (*bhay'upaṭṭhānañāṇa*)
7. Knowledge of Contemplation of Danger (*ādīnavānupassanāñāṇa*)
8. Knowledge of Contemplation of Disenchantment (*nibbidānupassanāñāṇa*)
9. Knowledge of Desire for Deliverance (*muñcitukamyatāñāṇa*)
10. Knowledge of Contemplation of Reflection (*paṭisankhānupassanāñāṇa*)
11. Knowledge of Equanimity about Formations (*sankhār'upekkhāñāṇa*)
12. Knowledge in Conformity with Truth (Conformity Knowledge) (*saccānulomikañāṇa*)
13. Knowledge of Change-of-Lineage (*gotrabhūñāṇa*)
14. Knowledge of Path (*maggañāṇa*)
15. Knowledge of Fruit (*phalañāṇa*)
16. Knowledge of Reviewing (*paccavekkhaṇañāṇa*).

The series of knowledges arises when the firm and concentrated mind is kept focused on the meditation subject. The first knowledge to arise, the Knowledge of Delimitation of Mind-and-Matter, is obtained with the completion of the first three purifications (i.e. Purification of Virtue, Purification of Mind and Purification of View). It is by bringing this first knowledge to maturity in three ways—internally, externally, and both internally and externally—that the Purification of View is completed. Purification of View is implicit in the Knowledge of Delimitation of Mind-and-Matter, and is reached on attaining this knowledge. But as yet the insight knowledges proper (*vipassanāñāṇa*) have not arisen. The insight knowledges are ten in number, ranging from the Knowledge by Comprehension to Conformity Knowledge. They are founded upon the Purification of View and Purification by Overcoming Doubt, which in turn are founded upon the two roots, Purification of Virtue and Purification of Mind.

To attain the Knowledge of Delimitation of Mind-and-Matter, the meditator, having purified his mind through the successful practice of concentration, focuses his attention on his meditation subject, which could be a hair, a skeleton, the rising and falling movements of the abdomen (i.e. the wind-element as a tactile object), or mindfulness of breathing. As he goes on attending to that meditation subject, he begins to understand it as consisting of two aspects—a material aspect and a mental aspect, together called "mind-and-matter" (*nāma-rūpa*).

As a rule, one first becomes aware of those parts pertaining to the material aspect of the meditation subject. Whatever parts pertain to its mental aspect attract one's attention later. But sometimes both the mental and material aspects become manifest to the meditator at once. The meditator may even feel that the meditation subject is actually impinging on his mind.

In mindfulness of breathing, for instance, the in-breaths and out-breaths belong to matter while the awareness of them is reckoned as mind. Normally, the in-breaths and the out-breaths strike against the tip of the nose or the upper lip as they enter and go out. The meditator should pay attention only to the occurrence of in-breathing and out-breathing. He should not follow the in-breaths inside the body or outside it, speculating on what becomes of them, since this will hinder concentration. As the meditator continues to keep his calm mind on the point of contact of the air being inhaled and exhaled (i.e. either at the tip of the nose or on the upper lip), he begins to feel as though his mind approaches and strikes the meditation subject. This happens at a developed stage in his meditation when he becomes aware of the distinction between mind and matter. The mind has the nature of bending towards or leaping towards an object. At first, every in-breath and out-breath appears as a compact unit. Later one begins to understand that the breath is a mass or heap. This is Delimitation of Matter. One then understands the awareness of the breath to be a series or "heap" of discrete thought-moments, each one a "heap" or mass of many mental factors. This is Delimitation of Mind. The ability to understand Mind-and-Matter as a heap necessarily implies the ability to distinguish one thing from another, since a heap is, by definition, a group of things lying one on another.

This is the preliminary stage of the Knowledge of Delimitation of Mind-and-Matter. At first this understanding is limited to the subject of meditation. Later on it spreads to the other parts of the body connected with the subjects of meditation until it comes to pervade the entire body. Still later the understanding extends outward towards other beings as well as inanimate things, since the knowledge, when complete, is threefold: internal, external, and internal-and-external.

CHAPTER IV

PURIFICATION BY OVERCOMING DOUBT
(*Kankhāvitaraṇavisuddhi*)

During the time of the Buddha there were ascetics who had raised such sceptical doubts about life as: "From where has this being come?" "What is his destiny?" etc. Even among those who could recollect their previous lives there were some who constructed misleading speculative theories. Some who had gained recollective knowledge and could see a limited number of their past lives went on to fabricate various speculative views concerning the past that lay beyond their ken. Thus there were theories of a soul and of a creator God, as well as views denying causality and conditionality. Owing to this diversity of views, sceptical doubt arises like the wavering in the mind of one who has reached a crossroad. The speculative views serve only to perpetuate that doubt.

These non-Buddhist ascetics had neither a Knowledge of Delimitation of Mind-and-Matter nor a Purification by Overcoming Doubt. They had attained jhāna basing their thoughts on the soul theory. Due to their lack of understanding, they misinterpreted their meditative experience and became entangled in doubts and wrong views.

To gain freedom from all doubts concerning the nature and pattern of existence, it is necessary to understand the law of cause and effect, clearly revealed to the world by the Buddha. This understanding is called the Knowledge of Discerning Cause and Condition (*paccayapariggahañāṇa*). With the maturing of this knowledge the Purification by Overcoming Doubt is brought to completion. Thus the second knowledge is obtained in the process of reaching the fourth purification. This Knowledge of Discerning Cause and Condition is also known as "knowledge of things-as-they-are" (*yathābhūtañāṇa*), "right vision" (*sammādassana*) and "knowledge of relatedness of phenomena" (*dhammaṭṭhitiñāṇa*). Some who have had experience in insight meditation in past lives are capable of discerning cause and condition immediately along with their discerning of mind-and-matter.

Owing to his Purification of View, the meditator goes beyond the perception of a "being" or "person." Advancing to the Purification by Overcoming Doubt, he begins to understand that consciousness always arises depending on a particular sense faculty and a sense object, that there is no consciousness in the abstract. As the Buddha says:

> Just as, monks, dependent on whatever condition a fire burns, it comes to be reckoned in terms of that condition—(that is to say), a fire that burns dependent on logs is reckoned as a "log-fire"; a fire that burns dependent on faggots is reckoned as a "faggot-fire"; a fire that burns dependent on grass is reckoned as a "grass-fire"; a fire that burns dependent on cow-dung is reckoned as a "cow-dung-fire"; a fire that burns dependent on rubbish is reckoned as a "rubbish-fire"—even so, monks, consciousness is reckoned by the condition dependent on which it arises. A consciousness arising dependent on eye and forms is reckoned as an "eye-consciousness"; a consciousness arising dependent on ear and sounds is reckoned as an "ear-consciousness"; a consciousness arising dependent on nose and smells is reckoned as a "nose-consciousness"; a consciousness arising dependent on tongue and flavours is reckoned as a "tongue-consciousness"; a consciousness arising dependent on body and tangibles is reckoned as a "body-consciousness"; a consciousness arising dependent on mind and ideas is reckoned as a "mind-consciousness."
>
> Mahātaṇhāsamkhaya Sutta
> M.I,259ff.

Thus the meditator understands that eye-consciousness arises because of the eye and a visual object, and that owing to eye-contact there arise feeling, perception, volition and thought. This is a twofold understanding as it concerns thought and its cause, feeling and its cause, perception and its cause, and so on. At this stage it occurs to him that there is no "I" or "person" apart from the four categories: mind and its cause, and matter and its cause.

The rise and fall of the abdomen now appear to him as an agglomeration of the wind-element. He recognizes the earth-element through the touch sensation at the tip of the nose together with the water-element associated with it. By means of the tactile sensation of warmth and coolness, he recognizes the fire-element. Now that the mind is free from the hindrances, there is ample scope for wisdom. He understands that matter also arises due to a cause. If the meditator is wise enough, he will understand that this birth has been brought about by some action (*kamma*) of the past, and that it is the outcome of craving, ignorance and grasping. Whatever creature he sees is, for him, just another instance of the four categories: mind and its cause, and matter and its cause.

At this stage one has to step-up one's practice of mindfulness and full awareness. In every instance of a change of posture one should make a mental note of the action, as well as of the intention which impelled that acton. The mental noting should always register the preceding thought as well:

1. 'intending to stand ... intending to stand'
2. 'standing ... standing'.

This method of making a mental note by way of cause and effect is helpful in understanding the relationship between the cause and the effect. The condition implied by the Knowledge of Discerning Cause and Condition is already found here. The meditator gradually comes to understand that thought is the result and that the object is its cause: "It is because there is a sound that a thought-of-hearing (an auditory consciousness) has arisen...."

As he goes on making a note without a break, a skilful meditator would even feel as though his noting is happening automatically. It is not necessary to make a special effort to increase one's understanding of mental objects in this way. One should rather understand the objects as and when they come. Any conscious attempt to accelerate the process would only distract the mind from the subject of concentration and thus retard the power of understanding. If the meditator is well read in the Dhamma, he will be able to gain a quicker understanding by reflecting according to the Dhamma. One who is not so well read will take more time to understand.

Some meditators gain the knowledge concerning the process of formations at the very outset. A meditator who is well advanced in regard to reflections on the Dhamma can arouse this knowledge while meditating on some subject of meditation, equipped with the Purification of Mind. This kind of knowledge is called the Knowledge of Discerning Mind-and-Matter together with Cause and Condition. That is, mind and matter are understood together with their cause and condition so that the knowledge of mind-and-matter and the knowledge of cause and effect arise simultaneously. By developing this knowledge, the Purification by Overcoming Doubt is attained.

One who has reached the stage of Purification by Overcoming Doubt clearly understands the three phases of the round of becoming—the cycle of defilements, the cycle of action, and the cycle of results:

> The cycle of defilements (*kilesavaṭṭa*) includes the defiling tendencies of the mind such as ignorance, craving, speculative views and grasping.
>
> The cycle of action (*kammavaṭṭa*) is the functional aspect of those defilements, that is, the mass of actions, both wholesome and unwholesome.
>
> The cycle of results (*vipākavaṭṭa*) consists in the pleasant and painful results of those actions.

This understanding is not based on assumptions. It is something that occurs to the meditator as an indubitable experience. At this stage although real insight still has not yet reached completion, the mind possesses great strength. This is a stage with special significance, since the meditator who has come this far becomes a "lesser Stream-enterer" (*culla-sotāpanna*). If he preserves this knowledge of conditionality intact up to the time of death, unimpaired by doubts and waverings, in his next existence he is certain not to be reborn into the four lower worlds: the hells, the world of afflicted spirits (*petas*), the animal kingdom, and the world of titans (*asuras*).

For one who already possesses the five direct knowledges (*abhiññā*)—(1) the knowledge of the modes of psychic power, (2) the divine ear-element, (3) the penetration of other minds, (4) the knowledge of recollecting past lives, and (5) the knowledge of the passing away and re-arising of beings—it is sometimes possible, on attaining this stage, to see past lives together with their causes and conditions. To some meditators, even the functioning of the internal organs of the body becomes visible. Some have visions of their childhood experiences. One who has no direct knowledge can also arouse memories of his childhood and past lives if he dwells immersed in meditation to the exclusion of all worldly concerns and extraneous thoughts.

Saṁsāra—the cycle of recurrent births and deaths—is perpetually kept in motion by speculative views and sceptical doubts. (See Sabbāsava Sutta, M.I,8.) With Purification of View, the mind gains purity by extricating itself from speculative views. With Purification by Overcoming Doubt, the mind becomes pure through the removal of sceptical doubts. The abandonment of views and sceptical doubts at this stage is done merely by the substitution of opposites (*tadangappahāna*). This abandonment by substitution of opposites is the abandoning of a particular unwholesome thought by means of an antithetical wholesome thought; it can be compared to the dispelling of darkness by lighting a lamp. The abandonment by suppression (*vikkhambhanappahāna*), accomplished through serenity meditation, is more effective. By means of this method one can sometimes keep the five hindrances suppressed even for a long time. The abandonment by cutting off (*samucchedappahāna*), accomplished by the supramundane path-knowledge, completely eradicates the defilements together with their underlying tendencies so that they will never spring up again.

In insight meditation, the underlying tendencies to speculative views and sceptical doubts still persist. They are abandoned as a "cutting off" only by the path of Stream-entry. The eradication of the underlying tendencies to defilements in such a way that they will never arise again is a distinctive quality of supramundane states.

The meditator engaged in cultivating virtue, concentration and wisdom should be as heedful in his task as a farmer diligently busying himself in cultivating his field. What has to be done today must not be postponed for tomorrow: "Procrastination is the thief of time." The first thing that gives trouble to a meditator sitting down to meditate is his own thoughts. The next troublemaker is pain. To combat thoughts, one has to be skilful in making a mental note of them. When the mind tries to play truant by leaving the meditation subject and going astray, one should make a mental note: 'Mind strays, mind strays.' If one goes on with mental noting throughout the day, one can, to a great extent, overcome stray thoughts. But pain is a far more formidable enemy. At first thoughts and pain both keep on troubling the meditator, but when meditation shows some signs of progress, pain appears as the more vicious of the two. Yet it has been a matter of experience that when meditation is well on its way to progress, one can even overcome severe pains which earlier seemed insurmountable. Therefore, understanding the secret of success well, one should make such a firm determination as: "I will not get up from this seat even if my bones break and the joints fall apart."[1]

Then the whole body will cool down, the pain will subside, and one will be able to go on sitting for a longer stretch of time. From that day onwards one will discover the ability to have longer sittings in meditation without pain. A meditator has to arouse the right amount of courage to overcome pain, thinking: "After all, this little suffering is not as oppressive as the suffering in hell." Or, "Let me suffer this little pain for the sake of the supreme bliss of Nibbāna." An example is the venerable Lomasanāga Thera who endured piercing cold and scorching heat. Once while he was dwelling in in the Striving-hall in Piyanga Cave at Cetiyapabbata, he spent wintry nights in the open air, reflecting on the sufferings in the inter-space hells, without losing his meditation subject. Again, in summer he spent the daytime sitting in the open air intent on his subject of meditation. When a pupil of his said: "Venerable sir, here is a cool spot. Please come and sit here," he retorted, "Friend, it is precisely because I am afraid of the heat that I sat here." And he continued sitting there having reflected on the burning heat in Avīci-hell.[2]

While engaged in insight meditation, attending mentally to sections of formations, a meditator sometimes goes through experiences which reveal to him the very nature of formations. While sitting in meditation his entire body stiffens: this is how the earth-element makes itself felt. He gets a burning sensation at the points of contact: this is a manifestation of the fire-element. He is dripping with sweat: this is an illustration of the water-element. He feels as if his body is being twisted: here is the wind-element at work. These are just instances of the four elements announcing themselves with a "here-we-are!" A meditator has to understand this language of the four elements.

---

1. "Let this body break up, if it must; let lumps of flesh lay scattered; let the pair of shins fall apart from my knee-joints."(Mudita Thera, Thag. v.312)

2. MA. Commentary on Sabbāsava Sutta.

CHAPTER V

PURIFICATION BY KNOWLEDGE AND VISION OF WHAT IS PATH AND NOT-PATH (*Maggāmaggañāṇadassanavisuddhi*)

The understanding of the distinction between the direct path and its counterfeit, the misleading path, is referred to as Purification by Knowledge and Vision of What is Path and Not-Path. When the meditator arrives at this stage, he has already passed four stages of purification. It is noteworthy that the last three purifications (i.e. Purification by Knowledge and Vision of What is Path and Not-Path, Purification by Knowledge and Vision of the Way, and Purification by Knowledge and Vision) have the qualification "Knowledge and Vision," unlike the first four. Hence Purification by Knowledge and Vision of What is Path and Not-Path marks a significant turning point in the ascent through the purifications and the knowledges.

By the time the meditator reaches this Purification by Knowledge and Vision of What is Path and Not-Path, he has gained a certain degree of clarity owing to his Purification by Overcoming Doubt. Since he has eliminated obstructive views and doubts, his power of concentration is keener than ever. Now his concentration has reached maturity. His mind is virile and energetic. He understands the nature of phenomena, manifest to him as mind-and-matter, together with their causes and conditions.

He has also gained two other significant advantages. The first is relief from stray thoughts, especially when he meditates without a break for the whole day; for such a meditator the stray thoughts arise only very rarely, and whereas earlier the stray thoughts that arose used to stay with him for a long while, now he can dismiss them summarily with a mere mental note. The second advantage is a significant reduction in the painful feelings that arise when sitting in meditation; to his great relief, the meditator finds that even though pains arise, he is now able to note them mentally without being distracted so that he can more easily keep his mind on the subject of meditation. Even severe pains now appear to him as normal events rather than disturbances. This is the "conquest of pain," a victory with a special significance.[1] With this new-found strength the meditator carries on mental noting with great precision. This stage marks the final phase of the Purification by Overcoming Doubt.

1. Knowledge by Comprehension
(*Sammasanañāṇa*)

Following the Purification by Overcoming Doubt, but preceding the next purification, Knowledge by Comprehension sets in, which in turn leads to Knowledge of Arising and Passing Away. Knowledge of Arising and Passing Away occurs in two phases: an undeveloped phase and a mature phase. In the undeveloped phase certain interesting phenomena occur to the meditator, encouraging in their own right but potential distractions from the correct path of practice; these are called the *ten imperfections of insight*. It is here that the Purification by Knowledge and Vision of What is Path and Not-Path comes in. This purification involves understanding that attachment to the ten imperfections of insight is the *not-path*, and that attending to the process of observation (i.e. mental noting) proper to the way of insight, is *the path*. It is so named because it purifies the person who attains it of the misconception that the not-path is the path.

Knowledge by Comprehension (also called Comprehension by Groups) is the reflection on formations in terms of their three universal characteristics—impermanence (*anicca*), suffering (*dukkha*), and not-self (*anattā*). Such reflection sets in between the Purification by Overcoming Doubt and the Purification by Knowledge and Vision of What is Path and Not-Path, but it does not fall into either of these two purifications by way of classification. The improvements in the meditator's ability help him in building up his Knowledge by Comprehension which brings the proper understanding of the three characteristics. But the range of comprehension this knowledge involves is not the same for everyone. For some meditators, the comprehension is broad and extensive; for others, its range is limited. The duration of the occurrence of this knowledge also varies according to the way the formations

1. In serenity meditation, sitting for three hours without being harassed by pain is regarded as the "conquest of pain."

relating to mind-and-matter are reflected upon. The Buddha's comprehension of formations pervaded all animate and inanimate objects in the ten thousand world-systems. The venerable Sāriputta's Knowledge by Comprehension pervaded everything animate and inanimate in the central region of India. The sutta expressions "all is to be directly known" (*sabbaṁ abhiññeyyaṁ*), and "all is to be fully known" (*sabbaṁ pariññeyyaṁ*) also refer to Knowledge by Comprehension. Here "all" (*sabbaṁ*) does not mean literally everything in the world, but whatever is connected with the five aggregates.

The formula of comprehension given in the suttas says:

> Any form whatever, whether past, future or present, internal or external, gross or subtle, inferior or superior, far or near—all form he sees with right wisdom as it really is (thus): "This is not mine," "This is not I am," "This is not my self." Any feelings whatever ... any perceptions whatever ... any formations whatever ... any consciousness whatever, whether past, future or present, internal or external, gross or subtle, inferior or superior, far or near—all consciousness he sees with right wisdom as it really is (thus): "This is not mine," "This is not I am," "This is not myself." (A.II,171)

Now, let us see how an ordinary meditator can apply this formula as a guide to comprehension. Suppose the meditator is keeping his mind on his meditation subject—mindfulness of breathing, the rise-and-fall of the abdomen, or something else. By now the subject of his meditation has gone beyond its conventional significance and is seen in terms of its ultimate constituents. For instance, if the meditation subject is a hair, it now manifests itself to him as the elements of earth, water, fire, air, colour, odour, flavour and nutritive essence. If the subject is mindfulness of breathing, it clearly appears as mind-and-matter together with their causes and conditions. Now, as the meditator goes on attending to his meditation subject, the arising and the passing away of those formations become apparent to him. He sees, as a present phenomenon, how the formations of mind-and-matter connected with his subject of meditation keep on arising and passing away and undergoing destruction—all in heaps. The understanding of formations as a heap is followed by the understanding of each of them separately. It is the continuity and compactness (*ghana*) of that which conceals the impermanence of formations.

To understand them separately, to see the discrete phases within the process, is to understand the characteristic of impermanence. The impermanence of formations becomes clear to him in accordance with the saying: "It is impermanent in the sense of undergoing destruction" (Ps.I,53). Once the nature of impermanence is apparent, the painful nature and not-self nature of formations become apparent as well.

When he makes a mental note of that understanding, the range of understanding itself grows wider. This is Knowledge by Comprehension, which comes as a matter of direct personal experience in the present. Based on this experience, he applies the same principle by induction to the past and the future. He understands by inductive knowledge that all formations in the past were also subject to destruction. When he understands the impermanence of past formations, he makes a mental note of this understanding as well. It also occurs to him that the same process will go on in the future. Thus he concludes that all formations in the three periods of time are indeed impermanent. He makes a mental note of this understanding too. As it is said: "Understanding conclusively past, future and present states (of the five aggregates) by summarisation (in groups) is Knowledge by Comprehension" (Ps.I,53).

All three characteristics become clear to him in this way: "It is impermanent because it wears away. It is painful because it is terrifying. It is not-self because it is coreless." At the stage of the Knowledge by Comprehension, the functioning of the mind is extremely rapid.

The three modes of comprehension—by way of past, future and present—are themselves sufficient for breaking up the defilements. However, eight additional modes have been indicated, grouped into four pairs: (1) internal-external, (2) gross-subtle, (3) inferior-superior, (4) far-near.

These eight modes are not apprehended by everyone in the course of reflection on formations. They occur with clarity only to those of keen insight. Together with the three temporal modes, these make up the eleven modes of comprehension indicated in the formula.[2]

---

2. Those specialized in the Abhidhamma doctrine of "ultimate categories" (*paramattha-dhamma*) describe the section of formations according to the eleven modes given above. Others are unable to describe them in detail although they may comprehend the formations according to those modes.

When the meditator attends to his subject of meditation, the materiality connected with it is comprehended by way of the eleven modes. So too are the associated mental aggregates—feeling, perceptions, mental formations and consciousness. Earlier, the meditator regarded consciousness as a compact unit, but now, as comprehension develops, he understands that there are thousands of thoughts—a heap of them occurring in a series, thought after thought. From this the meditator realizes that the thoughts arisen earlier are no longer present and with this conviction the perception of the compactness of consciousness loses its basis. Thus he awakens to the fact of impermanence. Feelings arising in the mind also become manifest as a heap—a series of distinct feelings flowing along without a pause. He becomes aware of the fact that a feeling disappears when he makes a mental note of it, and that along with it, the thought connected with the feeling also disappears. It now dawns on him that the "contact pentad" made up of contact, feeling, perception, volition and consciousness—the primary components of the mind (in mind-and-matter)—are all impermanent.

The meditator first has to reflect on his own set of five aggregates. At this stage his contemplation is not confined to his original meditation subject. Rather, contemplation pervades his entire body. He understands the nature of his whole body and makes a mental note of whatever he understands. This is comprehension. Not only in regard to his own body, but concerning those of others, too, he gains a similar understanding. He can clearly visualize his own body, as well as those of others, whenever he adverts to them. This is Knowledge by Comprehension.

Some meditators become acutely aware of the frail nature of their body as well. In the Discourse to Māgandiya, the Buddha gives the following advice to the wandering ascetic Māgandiya:

> And when, Māgandiya, you have practised the Dhamma going the Dhamma-way, then, Māgandiya, you will know for yourself, you will see for yourself, that these (five aggregates) are diseases, boils and darts. (M.I,512)

This again, is a reference to the above-mentioned stage of comprehension. In the Discourse to Dīghanakha, the Buddha expounded this method of comprehension in eleven ways:

> But this body, Aggivessana, which has material shape, is made up of the four great primaries, originating from mother and

> father, a heaping up of rice and rice-gruel, impermanent by nature, of a nature to be rubbed and massaged, fragile and perishable—this body should be regarded as impermanent, as painful, as a disease, a boil, a dart, a calamity, an affliction, as alien, as disintegrating, as void, as not-self.
>
> M.I,500

The Buddha indicated the method of comprehension in different ways, sometimes briefly, sometimes in detail, depending on the particular disciple's power of understanding. The Paṭisambhidāmagga gives forty modes of comprehension:

> [Seeing] the five aggregates as impermanent, as painful, as a disease, a boil, a dart, a calamity, an affliction, as alien, as disintegrating, as a plague, a disaster, a terror, a menace, as fickle, perishable, unenduring, as no protection, no shelter, no refuge, as empty, vain, void, not-self, as a danger, as subject to change, as having no core, as the root of calamity, as murderous, as to be annihilated, as subject to cankers, as formed, as Māra's bait, as subject to birth, subject to ageing, subject to illness, subject to death, subject to sorrow, subject to lamentation, subject to despair, subject to defilement.
>
> Ps.II,238

These forty modes can be distributed among the three characteristics as follows, ten illustrating the characteristic of impermanence, twenty-five the characteristic of suffering, and five the characteristic of not-self.

> Impermanence: impermanent, disintegrating, fickle, perishable, unenduring, subject to change, having no core, to be annihilated, formed, subject to death.
>
> Suffering: painful, a disease, a boil, a dart, a calamity, an affliction, a plague, a disaster, a terror, a menace, no protection, no shelter, no refuge, a danger, the root of calamity, murderous, subject to cankers, Māra's bait, subject to birth, subject to ageing, subject to illness, subject to sorrow, subject to lamentation, subject to despair, subject to defilement.
>
> Not-self: alien, empty, vain, void, not-self.

Out of these forty modes of comprehension, the meditator should reflect upon only those which make sense to him. There is no harm in not being able to understand every mode. It is enough if one reflects on those one can understand.

The meditator should understand exactly when this knowledge by comprehension becomes complete. Normally, there is a tendency to prolong the process of comprehension since one likes to go on reflecting in this way. For some meditators the process of comprehension reaches its culmination within a short period, for others it takes longer. When the Knowledge by Comprehension, starting from the meditation subject, extends to the five aggregates of the meditator, and from there to external formations, so much so that the three characteristics occur to him spontaneously and effortlessly in accordance with the norm of the Dhamma, and all animate and inanimate things appear to him as so many distinctive clusters of elements—then, at that stage the Knowledge by Comprehension can be regarded as complete.

When Knowledge by Comprehension develops to this stage, the meditator applies himself to meditation with great enthusiasm. He is even reluctant to get up from his meditation seat, as he feels he can continue reflecting on formations for a long time without any trouble. Sometimes he is totally free from thoughts about matters outside his meditation subject. By now, as the Comprehension-Knowledge is well developed, he clearly understands the three characteristics. The arising and passing away of formations is fully manifest to him. As he sees how each part arises and passes away, even such things as a flame of a lamp, a cascade of water, or a sound, appear to him as so many particles and heaps. The parts and particles of all these things become manifest to him as discrete but interconnected processes in the form of vibrations. They seem like a squirming swarm of worms. Even the body appears as a heap of fine elemental dust in constant transformation.

2. The Ten Imperfections of Insight
(*Dasa vipassan'upakkilesā*)

From the stage of Knowledge by Comprehension up to the initial phase of the Knowledge of Arising and Passing Away, the meditator becomes aware of an increasing ability to meditate without difficulty. Extraneous thoughts have subsided, the mind has become calm, clear and serene. Owing to this serenity and non-distraction, defilements decrease and the mental continuum becomes highly purified; the body, too, manifests the same serenity. As he is engaged in contemplation in the initial phase of the Knowledge of Arising and Passing Away, the meditator has to be extremely cautious. For it is precisely at this point that the *imperfections of insight* spring up, threatening to entice the unwary meditator away from the right path of practice. The *Visuddhimagga* (XX,105-125) describes ten such imperfections:

(1) illumination (*obhāsa*)
(2) knowledge (*ñāṇa*)
(3) rapturous delight (*pîti*)
(4) calmness (*passaddhi*)
(5) bliss (*sukha*)
(6) faith (*adhimokkha*)
(7) energy (*paggaha*)
(8) assurance (*upaṭṭhāna*)
(9) equanimity (*upekkhā*)
(10) attachment (*nikanti*).

(1) Due to the developed state of his mind at this stage, a brilliant light appears to the meditator. At first he catches a glimpse of something like a lamplight in the distance. Even if there is no lamp inside his hut, he seems to see one—even with his eyes open. He then discovers that this light emanates from his own body. Though his teacher had instructed him to simply make a mental note of everything he sees, the meditator now pays no heed to those instructions. He concludes that the teacher had not foreseen this event and was mistaken on this point. He even presumes that he is now more developed in meditation than his teacher. So he continues to enjoy the illumination without making a mental note of it. In such situations as these a meditator must not fall into delusion. The teacher's advice stems from the lineage of the Buddha and the Arahants. Therefore the meditator should regard his teacher's advice as if it were given to him by the Buddha himself and be diligent in making mental notes.

A skilful meditator endowed with discretion would be more cautious in a situation like this. He, too, first thinks that this illumination is a sign of some supramundane attainment. But he recognizes a desire for this illumination, and wisely reflects that that desire would not have arisen in him if he had actually attained a supramundane stage. So he concludes that this could not possibly be the path, and dismisses the illumination with a mental note. In the same way he becomes aware that craving arises whenever he thinks: "This is my illumination," and that conceit arises at the thought: "Even my teacher does not possess an illumination like mine." Also, in conceiving his experience to be a supramundane stage, he recognizes that he is holding a wrong view. So he refuses to be misled by the illumination and succeeds in abandoning this particular imperfection of insight.

(2) The same approach applies to the remaining imperfections. The meditator gains a remarkable insight into the meaning of canonical statements, doctrinal points and terms. Whatever words he reflects on now reveal to him a depth of meaning he had never previously seen in them. He mistakes this for discriminative wisdom (*paṭisambhidā*), and interpreting it as a supramundane quality, becomes enthusiastic in preaching. As a result, his meditation suffers a setback. This is the imperfection called "knowledge." The skilful meditator, however, who discerns the craving, conceit and views behind this imperfection, concludes that this is the not-path, abandons it, and moves on to the right path of mental noting.

(3) Because of his progress in comprehension, the meditator becomes transported with joy. Uplifting joy arises in him like heaving waves of the sea. He feels as though he is sitting in the air or on a cushion stuffed with cotton-wool. Here, again, the unskilful meditator is deceived. The skilful meditator, however, applies the same method of discernment as he did in the case of illumination. Regarding this imperfection as a manifestation of craving, conceit and wrong view, he frees himself from its deceptive influence.

(4) The fourth imperfection of insight is buoyancy of body and mind. Though the meditator had already experienced some calmness even in the initial stages of meditation, the calmness that sets in at the beginning of the Knowledge of Arising and Passing Away is of a much higher order. At times he wonders whether he has somehow risen up into the air. When he paces up and down, he feels as if the experience is happening spontaneously. The unskilled meditator is misled by these experiences into concluding this to be a supramundane quality, since it is the Arahants who can rise up into the air. The skilful meditator, on the other hand, recognizes the imperfection by the three criteria of craving, conceit and view, and is not misled.

(5) As he is contemplating arising and passing away, a sublime happiness pervades the meditator's body and mind. Uneasiness and pain disappear. Here, too, the unskilful meditator is deceived, while the skilful one recognizes the imperfection and overcomes it.

(6) Sometimes the meditator becomes inspired by an intense faith in the Triple Gem (the Buddha, the Dhamma and the

Sangha), in his meditation teacher and in his meditation subject. Enthusiasm overwhelms him, like a flood of water gushing forth from a dam. Ecstatic with inspiration, the meditator wants to spend most of his time worshipping and preaching. He feels impelled to write letters to his relatives instructing them in the Dhamma. Due to excessive faith, he even starts crying, which makes him seem ridiculous. This wave of enthusiasm is also an obstacle that must be checked by mental noting. Here, too, the skilful meditator reflects wisely and recognizing the imperfection, returns to the path.

(7) The meditator becomes aware of an intense energy within him. He does not feel sleepy as before. Though he is energetic, there is no restlessness in his mind. He can go on meditating for a long time at a stretch. The unskilful meditator mistakes this, too, to be a supramundane quality and falls into craving, conceit and view. This, again, blocks his progress in meditation.

(8) The meditator also discovers that mindfulness comes effortlessly. Whenever he focuses his attention on some object, mindfulness is already present there, almost automatically. Due to this effortless awareness called "assurance," the unskilled meditator imagines himself to possess the perfect mindfulness of the Arahants; thus he is deceived. The skilful meditator, on the other hand, recognizes the craving, conceit and view behind this idea and passes beyond it.

(9) Equanimity as an imperfection of insight is twofold: namely, equanimity in insight and equanimity in adverting. Here, equanimity means the ability to attend to the meditation subject without much effort. This is different from the equanimity spoken of in connection with feelings. Whereas earlier the meditator had to make a special effort in applying insight to various formations, at this stage he finds that insight is happening automatically, like the turning of a wheel. It is very easy for him now to carry on reflection as the mind almost leaps towards its object. Whatever he reflects upon occurs to him with remarkable clarity. When such mental concomitants as contact, feeling and formations become apparent by themselves from all sides, together with their characteristics such as impermanence, owing to his equanimity in adverting, it is easy enough for a meditator to mistake this for a supramundane insight. What is not so easy is to remain undeceived. But here, too, the skilful meditator succeeds in overcoming this imperfection of insight.

(10) The subtle imperfection of insight called "attachment" is one which is latent in all other imperfections. The unskilful meditator conceives a subtle attachment to his insight which is adorned with such marvellous things as illumination; thus he is carried away by craving, conceit and view. The skilful meditator uses his discerning wisdom and frees himself from the influence.

3. The Path and the Not-Path

The diligent meditator should carefully make a mental note of all the imperfections of insight whenever they arise. Meditators who neglect this precaution, thinking: "After all, these are good things," will ultimately find themselves in difficult straits, unable to advance in meditation. Therefore one should do well to follow here the advice of one's teacher. One has to recognize all these as obstacles and dismiss them. For all these imperfections of insight have a subtle trace of attachment hidden beneath them, and thus they will deflect one from the right path. The understanding that these imperfections are not the right path and that the avoidance of them will lead one to the path is called Purification by Knowledge and Vision of What is Path and Not-Path. Thus the not-path is the tendency to come under the sway of the imperfections of insight and to go on meditating while obsessed by them. The right path is the elimination of those imperfections and the stepping on to true insight, that is, to the highroad of mental noting. At the end of this purification the mature phase of Knowledge of Arising and Passing Away sets in to begin the next purification.

CHAPTER VI

PURIFICATION BY KNOWLEDGE AND VISION OF THE WAY
(*Paṭipadāñāṇadassanavisuddhi*)

1. The Three Full Understandings
(*Pariññā*)

In the course of developing insight meditation, a meditator passes through three mundane (*lokiya*) stages of realization before he reaches the level of the supramundane (*lokuttara*). These three stages, called the mundane full understandings, are designated:

(1) full understanding as the known (*ñātapariññā*),

(2) full understanding as investigating (*tīraṇapariññā*),

(3) full understanding as abandoning (*pahānapariññā*).

(1) The plane of *full understanding as the known* extends from the Knowledge of Delimitation of Mind-and-Matter through the Knowledge of Discernment of Conditions. The function exercised in this stage is the understanding of the individual nature of phenomena. In brief this understanding extends simply to the salient characteristics of phenomena. Thus the meditator understands that the earth-element has the characteristic of hardness, the water-element that of trickling, the fire-element that of heat, the air-element that of distending, the mind that of cognizing, feeling that of being felt, and so on. In detail it covers the four defining modes of any phenomena: its characteristic, function, manifestation and proximate cause. The full understanding as the known enables the meditator to grasp the essential nature of phenomena, which it presents in terms of ultimate categories.

(2) Full understanding as the known provides the basis for the next stage, *full understanding as investigating*, which extends from Comprehension by Groups through the Knowledge of Arising and Passing Away. At this stage the meditator advances from discern-

ing the specific nature of individual phenomena to discerning their general nature—the marks of impermanence, suffering and not-self.

(3) *Full understanding as abandoning*, the highest mundane stage of realization, involves the systematic abandoning of defilements by the substitution of opposites (*tadangappahāna*), i.e. by the development of particular insights which eclipse defiled erroneous notions from the mind. This stage starts from the Knowledge of Dissolution and culminates in the Knowledge of Equanimity about Formations. In this stage, as the ignorance obscuring the true nature of formations dissolves and things are seen for what they are, defilements begin to be dispersed. They are compelled to quit the recesses of the mind, and the more they vacate, the more strength of understanding the mind gains.

A meditator will find it useful to bear in mind this threefold division of mundane full understanding and its relation to the purifications and the stages of knowledge.

2. The Progress of Insight Knowledge

When the meditator steers clear of the ten imperfections of insight and returns to his mental noting, he completes Purification by Knowledge and Vision of What is Path and Not-Path. He then enters the mature phase of the Knowledge of Arising and Passing Away. With this he begins the last of the mundane purifications, Purification by Knowledge and Vision of the Way. The "way" signifies the practice or the process of arriving at the goal. The understanding, knowledge, or illumination relating to the process of arrival is the Knowledge and Vision of the Way. The purification or elimination of defilements by means of that knowledge is Purification by Knowledge and Vision of the Way. It is at this point that there begins to unfold the series of full-fledged insight knowledges which will climax in the attainment of the supramundane paths.

Purification by Knowledge and Vision of the Way comprises eight stages of knowledge:

1. Knowledge of Contemplation of Arising and Passing Away (*udayabbayānupassanāñāṇa*)
2. Knowledge of Contemplation of Dissolution (*bhangānupassanāñāṇa*)

3. Knowledge of Appearance as Terror (*bhay'upaṭṭhānañāṇa*)
4. Knowledge of Contemplation of Danger (*ādīnavānupassanāñāṇa*)
5. Knowledge of Contemplation of Disenchantment (*nibbidānupassanāñāṇa*)
6. Knowledge of Desire for Deliverance (*muñcitukamyatāñāṇa*)
7. Knowledge of Contemplation of Reflection (*paṭisankhānupassanāñāṇa*)
8. Knowledge of Equanimity about Formations (*sankhār'upekkhāñāṇa*).

Knowledge in Conformity with Truth or Conformity Knowledge (*anulomañāṇa*) is also included in this purification as a ninth stage of knowledge.

(1) *Knowledge of Contemplation of Arising and Passing Away.* Purification by Knowledge and Vision of the Way starts with the mature phase of the Knowledge of Arising and Passing Away, which sets in after the meditator has dispelled the deception posed by the imperfections of insight, either through his own unaided efforts or with the help of the teacher's instructions. He obtains this purification in the course of reflecting on his meditation subject with the pure undeluded mind now well on its way to true insight.

The Knowledge of Contemplation of Arising and Passing Away is defined thus: "The wisdom in contemplating the change of present phenomena is the Knowledge of Contemplation of Arising and Passing Away" (Ps.I,1). It is by contemplating formations as present phenomena that this particular knowledge is attained. Before this, the reflection on formations took stock of all three temporal modes—past, present and future; but now it is concentrated only on the present. This is a necessary step for seeing the change of formations, i.e. the alteration of the present condition. In order to see impermanence, one has to perceive the characteristic of passing away, and for passing away to be seen, the event of arising must also be seen. The Knowledge of Arising and Passing Away involves the seeing of both arising and dissolution. At this stage, the process of arising and dissolution becomes manifest to the meditator in the very subject of meditation he has taken up.

Now that he has passed the dangers posed by the imperfections of insight, the meditator proceeds with greater determination in his work of contemplation. All the three characteristics of existence now become clear to him in a reasoned manner. Though these characteristics appeared to him already in the early phase of the Knowledge of Arising and Passing Away, they were not so clear then because of the adverse influence of the imperfections. But with the imperfections gone, they stand out in bold relief.

Since the highroad of insight knowledge begins with the Knowledge of Arising and Passing Away, the meditator should be especially acquainted with this particular knowledge. He requires a thorough understanding of the three characteristics—impermanence, suffering and not-self. Each of these has two aspects:

(1) that which is impermanent and the characteristic of impermanence;

(2) that which is suffering and the characteristic of suffering;

(3) that which is not-self and the characteristic of not self.

The referent of the first set of terms—i.e. *that which* is impermanent, suffering and not-self—is the five aggregates. The characteristic of impermanence is the mode of arising and passing away; the characteristic of suffering is the mode of being continually oppressed; the characteristic of not-self is the mode of insusceptibility to the exercise of power. The five aggregates are thus impermanent because they arise and pass away, suffering because they are continually oppressed, and not-self because there is no exercising power over them. The *Paṭisambhidāmagga* explains the three characteristics thus: "(It is) impermanent in the sense of wearing away. (It is) suffering in the sense of bringing terror. (It is) not-self in the sense of corelessness" (Ps.I,53).

All the three characteristics are to be found in the five aggregates. The aim of the insight meditator should be to arouse within himself an understanding of these three characteristics. This kind of effort might appear, at first sight, as a mental torture. But when one considers the solace which this beatific vision yields, one will realize that in all the three worlds there is no worthier aim than this. As the Buddha says: "To that monk of serene mind who has entered an empty house and sees with right insight the Dhamma, there arises a sublime delight transcending the human plane" (Dhp.373).

The characteristic of impermanence is concealed by continuity. The characteristic of suffering is covered up by the change of postures. The characteristic of not-self is overcast with compactness.

The process of formations needs to be analyzed. Once it is seen as a heap or series, impermanence is understood. By resisting the impulse to change one's postures, suffering is understood. By analyzing the mass of formations into its constituents—earth, water, fire, air, contact, feeling, etc., the characteristic of not-self becomes evident. When these three characteristics become clear to the meditator, he is in a position to carry on his meditation well.

As the meditator goes on attending to his meditation subject, the subject begins to appear to him as clearly as it did at the stage of comprehension. Now, when the formations which make up mind-and-matter become manifest to him, he is able to distinguish the material and mental components of his meditation subject. If, for example, he takes the rise and fall of the abdomen as his subject, he comes to understand that within one rising movement of the abdomen there is a multiplicity of such movements and that within one falling movement there is also a series of similar movements. He can also see mentally that a series of thoughts arises along with this process, taking each fractional movement as object. If he attends to the in-breathing and out-breathing as the subject of his meditation, he can mentally distinguish between the numerous phases of the wind-element connected with the process. He is also aware that a series of thoughts arises, cognizing each phase.

When he is able to distinguish in this manner, his mind traverses his entire body, making it the subject of meditation. He understands that his entire body is a heap of elemental dust. It occurs to him that this heap of elemental dust composing his body is always in a state of motion, like the fine dust motes seen floating in the air when viewed against the sun's rays. At this stage his mind does not wander towards other objects. His attention is now fully engrossed in meditation. When he becomes aware of the components of matter and mind as heaps, series or masses, he begins to see the arising and the passing away of those distinct parts.

Here, one has to take into account another important fact, namely, that all the phenomena subsumed under mind-and-matter pass through three stages: (1) arising (*uppāda*), (2) persistence (*ṭhiti*), and (3) dissolution (*bhanga*). Birth, decay and death occur even within a very short period of time just as much as within the duration of a long period. Of these three stages, "arising" or "birth" and "dissolution" or "death" are apparent. The intermediate stage of "persistence" or "decay" is not so clear. "Arising" is the beginning of impermanence, "persistence" its middle and "dissolution" its end.

The three characteristics—impermanence, suffering and not-self—are now very clear to the meditator. Impermanence is mentally discernible to him as if it were something visible to his very eyes. Four things appear with clarity before his calm mind: (1) the arising, (2) the cause of arising, (3) the dissolution, (4) the cause of dissolution. The knowledge which arises together with this clarity of vision is the Knowledge of Arising and Passing Away. At whatever moment this knowledge dawns upon a meditator at an experiential level as a "realisation," he should do well to stop at that point for a considerable period of time in order to reflect upon it over and over again. The Knowledge of Arising and Passing Away is a significant starting-post. Since greater acquaintance with it will come in useful to a meditator even in the matter of re-attaining to fruition (*phalasamāpatti*), one can contemplate with the Knowledge of Arising and Passing Away even a hundred or a thousand times.

Now, the meditator who has developed the Knowledge of Arising and Passing Away and repeatedly practised it, directs his mind to his subject of meditation. The process of arising and passing away then becomes manifest to him in that very subject. Even in raising his arm and putting it down, he can visualize the beginning, the middle and the end of the process of arising and passing away. But sometimes the middle is not clearly discernible. This is also so in the case of the rising and falling movements of the abdomen. In mindfulness of breathing, the beginning, the middle and the end of the in-breaths and the out-breaths are apparent. The mind does not wander. As the meditator continues to keep his meditative attention on the meditation subject, after some time the beginning and the middle stages of the process seem to disappear. Only its end is apparent. When attending to the rising movement of the abdomen, the beginning and the middle become almost indiscernible. Only the end is apparent. So also in the case of the falling movement of the abdomen. In raising the arm and lowering it or in lifting the foot and putting it down, the beginning and the middle are not apparent. Only the end of each process stands out. In the case of the in-breaths and the out-breaths, the incoming and the out-going are not felt. All that the meditator feels is the touch sensation left by the in-breaths and the out- breaths at the tip of the nose or on the upper lip where they normally strike as they pass. And this is so palpable to him that he can almost hear its rhythm—"tuck-tuck-tuck." He is not aware of any other object.

Sometimes a meditator, on reaching this stage, might think that his meditation has suffered a setback since the meditation subject is no longer clear to him. He even stops meditating. If he is meditating under a teacher, he approaches him and complains about the setback he is faced with. He confesses that he has lost his interest in meditation—that he is fed up with it. The teacher, however, points out, with due reasons, that this is not a setback in meditation, but rather a sign of progress: "At the start, you had taken up the subject of meditation in terms of signs and modes. A 'mode' is a 'model.' All these meditation subjects—in-breathing and out-breathing, hairs, fingers, etc.—are mere concepts. Now that you have developed your mindfulness and concentration, your wisdom has also developed. By developed wisdom a non-existing sign is understood as non-existing. So you must not be disappointed. This is how the perception of the compact disappears."

The perception of the compact (*ghana-saññā*) is the tendency to take as a unity what is really a multiplicity of actions and functions. Compactness is fourfold:

(1) compactness as a continuity (*santati-ghana*)

(2) compactness as a mass (*samūha-ghana*)

(3) compactness as a function (*kicca-ghana*)

(4) compactness as an object (*ārammaṇa-ghana*).

At the developed stage of insight meditation, the perception of compactness begins to disintegrate. The rising and falling movements of the abdomen become less and less palpable. One loses awareness of one's entire body. Earlier the meditator could visualize his own body in the seated posture, but now even that becomes imperceptible to his mind. This is the point at which the concept breaks up. Here one has to abide by the teacher's instructions and be diligent in practice.

In his everyday life, man depends on a multitude of concepts of conventional origin. When the perception of compactness disintegrates, conventional notions also break up. One is beginning to move from the fictions believed by the deluded to the truths seen by the noble ones: "Whatever, monks, has been pondered over as truth by the world with its gods and Māras, by the progeny consisting of recluses and brahmins, gods and men, that has been well discerned as untruth by the noble ones as it really is with right wisdom—this is one mode of reflecting. And whatever, monks, has been pondered over as untruth by the world with its gods and Māras ... that has been discerned as truth by the noble ones as it really is with right wisdom—this is the second mode of reflection" (Dvayatānupassanā Sutta, Sn.147).

(2) *Knowledge of Contemplation of Dissolution.* When the meditator no longer sees the arising of formations and only their dissolution is manifest to him, he has arrived at the Knowledge of Dissolution. Resuming his meditation after this experience, he sees the formations making up mind-and-matter to be constantly disintegrating, like the bursting of water bubbles or like froth boiling over from a pot of rice. He comes to understand that there is no being or person, that there are only mere formations always disintegrating.

While this Knowledge of Dissolution is going on within him, the meditator has the extraordinary experience of being able to see the thought with which he reflected on dissolution. Then he reflects on that thought as well. Thus he enters upon a special phase of powerful insight known as reflective insight (*paṭivipassanā*); it is also called insight into higher wisdom (*adhipaññā vipassanā*). As the *Paṭisambhidāmagga* says: "Having reflected on an object, he contemplates the dissolution of the thought which reflected on the object. The appearance (of formations) is also void. This is 'insight into higher wisdom'" (Ps.I,58). After reflecting on an object representing mind-and-matter, the meditator reflects upon the reflecting thought itself. Thus he now sees dissolution not only in every immediate object he adverts to, but in every thought he happens to think as well.

(3) *Knowledge of Appearance as Terror.* When everything coming under mind-and-matter is seen to be disintegrating, the meditator feels as though he is in a helpless condition. Since the mind-body process to which he has been clinging is seen to be breaking up, he gets alarmed to an unusual degree. Witnessing the dissolution of everything he has been depending on, terror arises in him as he fails to find any shelter or refuge anywhere. This

knowledge of fearfulness is technically called the Knowledge of Appearance as Terror. When this knowledge arises, the meditator should make a mental note of his experience of terror. Otherwise this terror will continue to haunt him. Being unable to put an end to it, he will find it difficult to proceed with his meditation. So at this point, too, it is essential to make a mental note.

(4) *Knowledge of Contemplation of Danger*. The understanding dawns that the entire gamut of saṁsāric existence in the three realms throughout the three periods—past, future and present—is subject to the same dissolution. With this insight, the knowledge of terror gives rise to an awareness of the dangers of formations. This is called the Knowledge of Contemplation of Danger. To understand the dangers of formations is to understand that they are wretched from beginning to end. The meditator sees no advantage whatsoever in the entire mass of formations. They appear to him only as a heap of dangers which present no choice between a desirable and an undesirable section. He feels as though he has come upon a thicket infested with furious leopards and bears, reptiles and robbers.

With this understanding of the danger, dispassion arises. The meditator gets disgusted with all formations. He thinks: "How much suffering have I undergone in the past for the sake of this tabernacle? How much more have I to endure just to perpetuate this frame of formations?" The passage from the knowledge of the dissolution to this experience of disenchantment is the powerful phase of insight meditation. The knowledges in this series arise almost simultaneously. Immediately with the knowledge of dissolution, the knowledges of terror, of danger and of disenchantment arise. Hence this entire series is sometimes simply termed "disenchantment."

Whenever a meditator finds that the knowledge of dissolution has arisen within him, he should make it a point to stick to his meditation seat, even if it means foregoing meals and refreshments. He should continue to sit motionless, allowing the cycle of insight knowledges to turn full circle. Those of keen insight pass through these stages very rapidly.

(5) *Knowledge of Contemplation of Disenchantment.* When the dangers in formations are understood, disenchantment sets in without any special effort. This knowledge of disenchantment, arisen through dissatisfaction with formations, is a kind of knowledge with which a meditator has to be well acquainted. The dis-

satisfaction is aroused by perceiving the dangers in formations. Initially it concerns the formations connected with the particular subject of meditation. However, when this knowledge is well developed, whatever occurs to the meditator arouses only disenchantment, whether it be his own five aggregates or those of others. All objects and places, all kinds of becoming, generation and destiny, and all stations of consciousness and abodes of beings appear in a way that heightens this disenchantment. At first the insight meditator has been thinking only of winning freedom from possible rebirth in the four planes of misery—the hells, the animal realm, the plane of afflicted spirits (*petas*), and the planes of titans (*asuras*). But now, because of this dissatisfaction with regard to formations by understanding their dangers, he is disgusted not only with the four lower planes but with all the three realms of existence: the sense-sphere realm, the fine-material realm and the immaterial realm. He cannot see any solace anywhere—not even in the heavens and Brahma worlds—since all formations appear as fearful.

When this dissatisfaction becomes acute, very often a meditator gets whimsical ideas which can be detrimental to his practice. He becomes dissatisfied with his meditation and meditates without relish. He thinks of stopping his meditation and going somewhere else. He even develops a dislike towards his teacher and other elders who seek his welfare. In view of this situation, it is advisable for a meditator intending to take up insight meditation to inform his meditation teacher or any other elder about his intention. Failing that, he should at least make a firm determination well beforehand to withstand the obstacles that might confront him in the course of insight meditation. For even after reaching this stage of disenchantment, one has to proceed further.

In such cases the meditation teacher, too, must be resourceful. He should recognize that the real source of the meditator's dissatisfaction is his insight into the dangers of formations, and that this discontent has only been displaced and transferred to other things. When a meditator comes and complains about his practice, place of residence, etc., the teacher must use skilful means to dispel his despondency and re-arouse his ardour for meditation. It is a good sign that, despite his problems, the meditator does not altogether give up his meditation.

(6) *Knowledge of Desire for Deliverance.* The Knowledge of Disenchantment is followed by the Knowledge of Desire for Deliv-

erance. The meditator now becomes desirous of being delivered from all the planes of becoming, destiny and generation found in all the three realms. He desires deliverance from all formations and thinks: "How shall I escape from this entire mass of formations bound up with defilements?"

Some peculiarities are noticeable in the meditator now, not present in the earlier stage. He is always reflecting on his own shortcomings. He does not stick to his meditation subject. He becomes restless and never feels at ease. For a while he gets up from the meditation seat and starts pacing up and down. Then again he comes and sits down. He turns his meditation seat to face another direction. He keeps on folding his robes several times and thinks of changing his requisites. Various plans for renovating his compound and even for changing the attitudes of other people enter his mind. But still he does not stop his meditation. However, in a situation like this, a meditator has to be extremely careful, otherwise his meditation is likely to suffer a setback. He should understand that all these whims and fancies are transient. If some impulse to leave his meditation seat arises at an unusual hour, he should make a mental note of it and refuse to respond to it. The meditator should form a resolve to be firm in dealing with these whimsical ideas of changing postures, requisites, etc., until he has gotten over this lapse—whether it lasts for a few minutes or continues for a number of hours or days.

(7) *Knowledge of Contemplation of Reflection.* Once he has recovered from this lapse, the meditator's powers of reflection increase and he passes through a series of important insights. These insights are classified into several groups, the most comprehensive being the *eighteen principal insights;* a set *of forty modes of reflection* also occurs to him with clarity.[1] Sometimes only a few of these insights and modes are conspicuous. As his understanding by means of mental noting progresses, the mind engaged in noting gets keener. The task before the meditator now is the comprehension of the five aggregatesof clinging as impermanent, suffering and not-self. The eighteen principal insights and the forty modes of reflection can all be distributed among these three characteristics. Every one of the above contemplations disperses the defilements by the method of "substitution of opposites." Along with this process of elimination, the Knowledge of Desire for De-

1. For the eighteen principal insights see Appendix 2; for the forty modes of reflection see p.34 above

liverance reaches maturity. The meditator becomes more enthusiastic in developing insight and carries on contemplation through the principal insights and modes of reflection. This kind of reflection is called Knowledge of Contemplation of Reflection or "Reflective Insight."

At the stage of the Knowledge of Reflection, insight tends to become renewed. Some unusual physical pains may occur when one reaches this stage. One may suffer severe headaches and a feeling of heaviness in the head, clumsiness of body or giddiness or drowsiness. One should, however, mentally note these painful feelings with diligence and try to bear up under them. Then those pains will gradually subside, so much so that one will be relieved of them until one reaches the very culmination of insight meditation. Sometimes pains arise due to physical causes such as ordinary illnesses. But even such pains, once they are overcome by sheer will-power, will not come up again. Sometimes this method even completely cures chronic ailments like headaches.

When the Knowledge of Reflection arises, insight has become highly developed. At this point it looks as though insight is about to reach its climax. This impels the meditator to make the firm determination: "Whatever there is to be done to win deliverance from existence, all that will I do."

(8) *Knowledge of Equanimity about Formations.*The next in the series of insight knowledges is Knowledge of Equanimity about Formations. The equanimity referred to results from a conviction that all the foundational work for uprooting the defilements has been accomplished and that no further effort is required in this direction. The knowledge of equanimity arises with the understanding of voidness (*suññatā*): that everything is void of self or what belongs to self. Since the meditator sees that there is neither a self nor anything belonging to a self in relation to himself as well as others, voidness is discerned in a fourfold manner:

(i) There is no "my self."

(ii) There is nothing belonging to "my self."

(iii) There is no "another self."

(iv) There is nothing belonging to "another self."

As the meditator goes on making a mental note of all that occurs to him in this manner, the mind engaged in observation becomes keener and keener until it reaches a stage of unruffled calm. At this stage, called "equanimity about formations," the meditator experiences no terror over the dissolution of formations, since he has discerned their ultimate voidness. Nor is there any delight regarding the keenness of reflection. As the *Visuddhimagga* says: "He abandons both terror and delight and becomes indifferent and neutral towards all formations" (XXI,61).

Reflection on formations now goes on effortlessly like a well-yoked chariot drawn by well-trained horses. The object presents itself to the reflecting mind without any special effort. It is as if the mind is propping up its objects. Just as water-drops fallen on a lotus leaf slide off at once, so distracting thoughts of love and hate do not stick to the meditator's mind. Even if an attractive or repulsive object is presented to him just to test his knowledge of equanimity about formations, it will simply roll away from his mind without stimulating greed or hatred. There is equanimity at this stage because the meditator understands objects in terms of the four elements. Owing to the absence of defilements, the meditator's mind seems pure like the mind of an Arahant, though at this point the suppression of defilements is only temporary, effected by the "substitution of opposites" through insight. It will be a great achievement if the meditator can continue to maintain this state of equanimity.

The *Paṭisambhidāmagga* defines the Knowledge of Equanimity about Formations thus:"Wisdom consisting of desire for deliverance together with reflection and composure is Knowledge of Equanimity about Formations" (Ps.I, 60f.). According to this definition, equanimity about formations has three stages: (1) desire for deliverance, (2) reflection, and (3) composure. Composure (*santiṭṭhāna*) is a significant characteristic of equanimity about formations. It implies the continuity of knowledge or the occurrence of series of knowledges as an unbroken process. No extraneous thoughts can interrupt this series. For a meditator who has reached this stage, very little remains to be done.

Some meditators are unable to go beyond the Knowledge of Equanimity about Formations due to some powerful aspirations they have made in the past, such as for Buddhahood, or Paccekabuddhahood, Chief Discipleship, etc. In fact, it is at this stage that one can ascertain whether one has made any such aspiration in the past. Sometimes when he has reached this stage the meditator himself comes to feel that he is cherishing a powerful aspiration. However, even for an aspirant to Buddhahood or

Paccekabuddhahood, the Knowledge of Equanimity about Formations will be an asset towards his fulfilment of the perfection of wisdom (*paññā-pāramī*). This Equanimity of Formations is of no small significance when one takes into account the high degree of development in knowledge at this stage.

(9) *Conformity Knowledge.* After Equanimity about Formations comes Knowledge in Conformity with Truth, or briefly, Conformity Knowledge. To gain this knowledge the meditator has nothing new to do by way of meditation; this knowledge simply arises by itself when Knowledge of Equanimity about Formations comes to full maturity. The function of Conformity Knowledge is to conform to the insights which had gone before, or to stabilise those gains by repeated practice. According to the *Visuddhimagga*, this conformity has to be understood in two senses: as conformity to the function of truth in the eight preceding kinds of insight knowledge, and as conformity to the thirty-seven requisites of enlightenment which are to follow soon.[2] When the eight preceding kinds of insight knowledge make their pronouncements like eight judges, Conformity Knowledge, like a righteous king, sits in the place of judgement and impartially and without bias conforms to their pronouncements by saying, "You have all discharged your duties well." And just as the judgement of a righteous king conforms with the ancient royal custom, so this Conformity Knowledge, while conforming to the eight kinds of knowledge, also conforms to the thirty-seven enlightenment factors, which are like the ancient royal custom (Vism. XXI, 130-133).

Though Knowledge of Equanimity about Formations is generally regarded as the culmination of Purification by Knowledge and Vision of the Way, it is Conformity Knowledge that imparts completeness to the Way. Purification by Knowledge and Vision of the Way may be said to have eight knowledges only in a qualified sense, since the last of them, Knowledge of Equanimity about Formations, includes Conformity Knowledge as well.

---

2. The thirty-seven requisites of enlightenment comprise: the four foundations of mindfulness, the four right endeavours, the four bases of spiritual power, the five spiritual faculties, the five spiritual powers, the seven enlightenment factors, and the eight noble path factors. For details see Ledi Sayadaw, *The Requisites of Enlightenment* (Wheel No. 171/174).

CHAPTER VII

PURIFICATION BY KNOWLEDGE AND VISION

(*Ñāṇadassanavisuddhi*)

With the completion of Knowledge of Equanimity about Formations, six stages of purification are complete. Purification by Knowledge and Vision, the seventh and final stage, comes next. This purification consists in the knowledge of the four supramundane paths. But before we discuss this directly, it is necessary to say a few things about the process immediately leading up to it.

1. Insight Leading to Emergence

(*Vuṭṭhānagāmini vipassanā*)

The most developed phase of the Knowledge of Equanimity about Formations is called *insight leading to emergence.* This insight brings one to the portal of the supramundane path. As this insight progresses, there arises the cognitive series (*cittavīthi*) heralding the supramundane path. Those of keen insight, when they reach Knowledge of Equanimity about Formations, fulfil at the same time the requirements for insight leading to emergence and at once pass through it to the supramundane paths and fruits. But the majority, when they reach this stage, go to the verge of Conformity Knowledge, and, unable to proceed further, come back to the Knowledge of Equanimity about Formations. This is illustrated in the *Visuddhimagga* by the simile of the crow:

> When sailors board a ship, it seems, they take with them what is called a "land-finding crow." When the ship gets blown off its course by gales and goes adrift with no land in sight, then they release the land-finding crow. The crow takes off from the masthead and after exploring all the quarters, if it sees land, it flies straight in the direction of it; if not, it returns and alights on the masthead. So too, if Knowl-

> edge of Equanimity about Formations sees Nibbāna, the state of peace, as peaceful, it rejects the occurrence of all formations and enters only into Nibbāna. If it does not see it, it occurs again and again with formations as its object.
>
> (Vism. XXI, 65)

If the meditator is well acquainted with the Dhamma and has discriminative wisdom, he will understand what has happened. Then he can again reflect on formations and go up to Conformity Knowledge.

By now the meditator has gained a good understanding of the nature of all compounded things (*sankhatadhammā*). So he is in a position to make an inference as to the nature of the Uncompounded (*asankhata*). There are three distinctive qualities of compounded things: (1) the impeding quality, (2) the signifying quality, and (3) the desiring quality.

Regarding the first of these, the meditator thinks: "Compounded things are bound up with impediments. Nibbāna, which I am seeking, is free from impediments." By "impediment" is meant something that has the nature of impeding. The impediments have the nature of causing a moral person to violate his moral precepts and of making him unrestrained; the nature of disrupting the concentration of one who is bent on attaining concentration and of driving him to distraction; and the nature of obscuring the wisdom of one who is developing wisdom and of casting him into delusion. Compounded things impede by way of lust, hatred, delusion, conceit, jealousy, views, and so on. In the Uncompounded there is no impediment whatsoever.

The main impediment is the personality view. One who is deceived by this view must abandon it. The impediment brought about by views can be eliminated only by getting rid of views. Nibbāna is free from the impediment of views. It is free from the impediment of uncertainty. In fact, it is free from all the impediments brought about by defilements.

The meditator now sees that all compounded things are oppressed by impediments. He feels that the day he is free from these compounded things he can attain Nibbāna.

As to the signifying quality, the meditator understands that all compounded things become manifest through signs and modes. Everything in mind-and-matter (*nāma-rūpa*) is defined by way of various modes, such as time, place, direction, occasion, colour, shape, etc. As the Buddha says:

> "If, Ānanda, all those modes, characteristics, signs and exponents by which there comes to be a designation of mind-and-matter were absent, would there be manifest any contact?"
>
> "There would not, Lord."
>
> "Wherefore, Ānanda, this itself is the cause, this is the origin, this is the condition for contact. That is to say, mind-and-matter."
>
> Mahā-Nidāna Sutta, D.II,62

Everything compounded rests on a mass of suffering: "The world rests on suffering" (S.I,40). The meditator understands that Nibbāna is free from suffering. Compounded things are liable to decay and death. In the Uncompounded there is no decay and death. The idea that Nibbāna is a tranquillization also occurs to the meditator now.

"Desire" means wish or longing. Compounded things cater to wishes. Their very existence is bound up with longing and desire. Food and drink, clothes and dwellings, the cake of soap, the razor and the broom—all these things are always in a process of wearing away. Various efforts are required to check this process of decay, and all these efforts are the outcome of longing. When one object of desire breaks up, man hankers for another. He goes on hankering like this because of the wish-begetting nature of compounded things and the nagging impulses they create.

When the meditator is in a position to infer that the Uncompounded is free from this characteristic, he is much relieved at heart. So he turns his attention to the Uncompounded, trying his best to attain it. Knowing well that the compounded is fraught with suffering, and that the Uncompounded is free from suffering, he puts forth the necessary effort with the determination: "Somehow I will attain it." It is when he makes such an endeavour that insight leading to emergence develops within him.

Insight leading to emergence is the climax of insight knowledge. This insight leads directly and infallibly to the supramundane path, referred to by the term "emergence." The insight leading to emergence comprises three kinds of knowledge: fully-matured knowledge of equanimity about formations, conformity knowledge, and change-of-lineage (still to be discussed). It covers the mundane moments of consciousness in the cognitive series issuing in the supramundane path—that is, the mind-moments called preliminary work (*parikamma*), access (*upacāra*), and conformity (*anuloma*). Since the phase of preliminary work has the task of attending to deficiencies in the balancing of the spiritual faculties, some meditators with sharp and well-balanced faculties skip this phase and go through only access and conformity. The rest must pass through all three. The mind at this stage is working with such rapidity that the entire process has to be reckoned in terms of thought-moments. (See Appendix 3.)

Up to the time of insight leading to emergence, the meditator had been contemplating the three characteristics of all formations—impermanence, suffering and not-self. As he continues reflecting on the three characteristics with keen insight, when he reaches insight leading to emergence, one characteristic stands forth more prominently than the others. Which one stands forth depends on his dominant spiritual faculty. One in whom faith is predominant will discern impermanence and subsequently apprehend Nibbāna as the signless (*animitta*); his path is called the signless liberation. One in whom concentration is predominant will discern the mark of suffering and apprehend Nibbāna as the desireless (*appaṇihita*); his path is called the desireless liberation. One in whom wisdom is predominant will discern the mark of not-self and subsequently apprehend Nibbāna as voidness (*suññatā*); his path is called the voidness liberation. The particular outstanding characteristic comes up distinctly in the most developed phase of knowledge of equanimity about formations, and persists as the mode of apprehension through three phases of insight leading to emergence: preliminary work, access and conformity.

2. Change-of-Lineage Knowledge
(*Gotrabhūñāṇa*)

During these three phases, the meditator's mind is working with formations as its object. He is seeing formations as impermanent, suffering or not-self. But with the next step, Change-of-Lineage Knowledge, a radical change takes place. As soon as Change-of-Lineage Knowledge occurs,the mind lets go of formations and takes Nibbāna as its object. This knowledge gains its name because at this point the meditator "changes lineage,"that is, he passes from the rank of a worldling (*putthujjana*) to the rank of a noble one (*ariya*). In the three phases preceding change-of-lineage the defilements continue to be abandoned temporarily through the substitution of opposites. Change-of-lineage itself does not directly abandon defilements in any way, but it heralds the onset of the supramundane path, which abandons defilements permanently by cutting off their roots.

According to the definition given in the *Paṭisambhidāmagga*, Change-of-Lineage Knowledge is the understanding of emergence and the turning away from the external. This knowledge emerges from formations as signs and turns away from their occurrence. The object of consciousness is twofold as sign (*nimitta*) and occurrence (*pavatta*). "Sign" is the mode, "occurrence" implies the occurring of defilements and formations. At the stage of change-of-lineage, consciousness abandons the sign so that almost automatically it becomes aware of that reality which is signless. In other words, it takes as its object Nibbāna. At this stage, defilements as such are not yet destroyed. But the tendency of the mind to grasp formations by means of signs and modes is discontinued and thus the signs associated with the defilements are transcended. This particular tendency had already been broken down to a great extent in the preceding course of insight meditation as, for instance, when breath becomes imperceptible and the consciousness of the body is lost. However, when the mind emerges from the sign at change-of-lineage, it is irreversible.

During the preceding stages of knowledge up to and including equanimity about formations, a fall away from onward progress is possible. But when change-of-lineage occurs, the attainment of the supramundane path is assured. Whereas preliminary work, access and conformity are mundane (*lokiya*) and the path and fruit supramundane (*lokuttara*), change-of-lineage has an intermediary position. The *Visuddhimagga* illustrates the transition to the path thus:

> Suppose a man wanted to leap across a broad stream and establish himself on the opposite bank, he would run fast and seizing a rope fastened to the branch of a tree on the stream's near bank and hanging down, or a pole, would leap with his body tending, inclining and leaning towards the opposite bank, and when he had arrived above the opposite bank, he would let go, fall on the opposite bank, staggering first and then steadying himself there; so, too, this meditator who wants to establish himself on Nibbāna, the bank

opposite the kinds of becoming, generation, destiny, station and abode, runs fast by means of the contemplations of rise and fall, etc., and seizing with conformity's adverting to impermanence, pain or not-self, the rope of materiality fastened to the branch of his selfhood and hanging down, or one among the poles beginning with feelings, he leaps with the first conformity-consciousness without letting go and with the second he tends, inclines and leans towards Nibbāna like the body that was tending, inclining and leaning towards the opposite bank; then being with the third next to Nibbāna, which is now attainable, like the others arriving above the opposite bank, he lets go that formation as object with the ceasing of that consciousness and with the change-of-lineage consciousness he falls on to the unformed Nibbāna, the bank opposite, but staggering as the man did, for lack of (previous) repetition, he is not yet properly steady on the single object. After that he is steadied (in Nibbāna) by Path Knowledge. (Vism.XXII,6)

3. The Supramundane Paths and Fruits

In the same cognitive series, immediately after the mind-moment of change-of-lineage comes the supramundane Path-Knowledge, followed directly by its corresponding fruition. Both the Path-Knowledge and Fruit-Knowledge take Nibbāna as their object.The path (*magga*) lasts for only a single moment of consciousness, whereas fruition (*phala*) occurs for either two or three mind-moments. For those of sharp faculties who skipped the phase of preliminary work, three moments of fruition occur; for others there are only two moments of fruition. All these events, the three preparatory moments, the path and fruition, belong to a single cognitive series called the "cognitive series of the path" because it brings the liberating knowledge of the path. After this cognitive series there occurs a fresh cognitive series which reviews the path attainment. This Reviewing-Knowledge takes formations as its object, not Nibbāna as do the paths and fruits. (See Appendix 3.)

Path-consciousness has the nature of emerging from both "sign" and "occurrence." "The understanding of emergence and turning away from *both* (i.e. from the 'occurrence' of defilements and from the 'sign' of aggregates produced by them) is knowledge of the path" (Ps.I,69). Up to this point the meditator had already become convinced that formations are painful and that their cessation, Nibbāna, is bliss. Now, with the path, he actually realizes this through direct seeing of Nibbāna. The *Paṭisambhidāmagga* says: "Seeing that formations are painful and that cessation is blissful is called the understanding of emergence and turning away from both (defilements and formations). That knowledge touches the Deathless State" (Ps.I, 70). The *Milindapañhā* describes the transition from insight contemplation of formations to the realization of Nibbāna by the path as follows: "That consciousness of his, while mentally traversing the range of reflection back and forth, transcends the continuous occurrence of formations and alights upon non-occurrence. One who, having practised rightly, has alighted upon non-occurrence, O King, is said to have realized Nibbāna" (p.326).

It is for the attainment of this supramundane path that the meditator has done all his practice. The aim of all his endeavours in fulfilling virtue and in developing meditation was the arousing of this path-consciousness. The path-consciousness accomplishes four functions in a single moment, one regarding each of the Four Noble Truths:

(1) it penetrates the truth of suffering by fully understanding it;

(2) it penetrates the truth of suffering's origin (craving) by abandoning it;

(3) it penetrates the truth of the path (the Noble Eightfold Path) by developing it;

(4) it penetrates the truth of suffering's cessation (Nibbāna) by realizing it.

This exercise of four functions simultaneously can be illustrated by the sunrise. With the rising of the sun, visible objects are illuminated, darkness is dispelled, light appears and cold is allayed. As the sun illuminates visible objects, so Path-Knowledge fully understands suffering; as the sun dispels darkness, so Path-Knowledge abandons the origin of suffering; as the sun causes light to be seen, so Path-Knowledge (as right view) develops the (other) path factors; as the sun allays cold, so Path-Knowledge realizes the cessation which is the tranquillization of defilements.

There are four supramundane paths which must be passed through to reach full purification and liberation: the path of

Stream-entry (*sotāpattimagga*), the path of Once-return (*saka-dāgāmimagga*), the path of Non-return (*anāgāmimagga*) and the path of Arahantship (*arahattamagga*). These four paths have to be attained in sequence. Attainment of all four can occur in a single life, or it can be spread out over several lifetimes; but once the first path is reached, the meditator is assured of never falling away and is bound to reach the final goal in at most seven lives.

Each path arises only once. Each has its own particular range of defilements to burst. When a path arises, immediately, by the power of knowledge, it bursts the defilements within its range. The first path, the path of Stream-entry, breaks the three fetters of personality view, doubt and clinging to rules and rituals. One who passes through this path and its fruition becomes a Stream-enterer (*sotāpanna*). He has entered the stream of the Dhamma, is forever liberated from the possibility of rebirth in the four lower planes (see above, p.26), and will be reborn at most seven more times in the human or heavenly worlds.

The second path, the path of Once-return, does not eradicate any defilements completely but greatly reduces the roots—greed, hatred and delusion. One who dies as a Once-returner (*sakadāgāmi*) will be reborn in the human world only one more time before attaining deliverance.

The third path, the path of Non-return, bursts the two fetters of sensual desire and aversion. One who passes away as a Non-returner (*anāgāmi*) will not be reborn at all in the sense-sphere realm; he is reborn only in the higher Brahma worlds where he attains final deliverance.

The fourth path, the path of Arahantship, eradicates the five subtle fetters—desire for fine-material existence (in the Brahma worlds), desire for non-material existence (in the formless worlds), conceit, restlessness and ignorance. The Arahant or liberated one is free from all bondage to *saṁsāra*. He lives in the full attainment of deliverance.

Purification by Knowledge and Vision, the seventh and last purification, consists in the knowledge of the four supramundane paths. Following each path, its own respective fruition occurs as its immediate result. Whereas the path performs the task of breaking up defilements, fruition experiences the bliss of Nibbāna when this demanding exertion subsides: "The understanding of the relaxation of endeavour is Knowledge of Fruition" (Ps.I, 71).

Since the fruition-consciousness immediately follows the

knowledge of the path without a time-lag, the path-concentration is called "concentration-with-immediate-result" (*ānantarika-samādhi*). This indescribably keen concentration enables wisdom to cut through the range of defilements and purify the mental-continuum. The *Paṭisambhidāmagga* states: "The understanding of the eradication of defilements owing to the purity of non-distraction is knowledge of concentration-with-immediate-result" (Ps.I, 71). The commentaries record that some held the view that Fruition-Knowledge arises a number of hours or days after Path-Knowledge; however, the term "with-immediate-result" (*ānantarika*) irrefutably conveys the sense of immediacy (literally, "without an interval"). Hence that dissentient view is groundless.

4. Reviewing Knowledge
(*Paccavekkhanañāṇa*)

After fruition there occurs Reviewing Knowledge. With this knowledge the meditator reviews five things: the path, its fruition, the defilements abandoned, the defilements remaining, and Nibbāna. Such is the case for Stream-enterers, Once-returners and Non-returners. But the Arahant has no reviewing of remaining defilements as he has cut them off entirely. Thus there is a maximum of nineteen reviewings, though some disciples may not review defilements abandoned and remaining. Some fail to undertake this reviewing immediately because of the exhilarating joy of attainment. However, they can review their attainment upon later reflection. The dissentient view that there is an interval between path-consciousness and fruition-consciousness could have arisen due to a misunderstanding of such instances of later recollection. The reviewing is not a deliberate act but something that occurs as a matter of course. Hence there is nothing wrong if it takes place afterwards.

With the attainment of the first three fruitions, the meditator, at the time of reviewing, gains the conviction that one essential part of his task is done. When the fruit of Arahantship is attained through the knowledge of the fourth path, he wins the blissful realization that his task has been fully accomplished: "He understands, 'Destroyed is birth, the holy life has been lived, what had to be done has been done, there is nothing further beyond this' " (M.I,41; M.L.S. I,p.50).

CONCLUSION

We have provided a general sketch of the Seven Stages of Purification and the sequence of insight knowledges. This is by no means a comprehensive survey of the field of meditation. At the outset of practice, a beginner must understand clearly the method of mental noting. Any laxity in this respect is bound to mar or retard one's progress in meditation. So one should pursue this practice of mental noting with faith and diligence. In all types of meditation, *mindfulness and full awareness should receive special attention.*

A meditator should not disclose to others his level of progress, for to proclaim one's attainments is normally due to defilements. However, for the purpose of getting instructions, one may disclose one's experiences to a suitable person, such as a teacher or an advanced practitioner.

In ancient times, to kindle a fire one had to go on rubbing two kindling-sticks together for a long time, unceasingly. If, after rubbing the sticks together a few times until they became a little warm, one stopped to rest, one had to start the process all over again. Therefore, to make a fire with kindling-sticks, one has to go on rubbing ceaselessly however long it might take until fire is produced. The meditator has to proceed in the same way. He cannot succeed if he practises by fits and starts. He must apply himself to meditation without a break until the Supreme Goal of his endeavour is realized.

> Knowing and seeing the eye, monks, as it really is, knowing and seeing forms as they really are, knowing and seeing eye-consciousness as it really is, knowing and seeing eye-contact as it really is, and knowing and seeing whatever feeling—pleasant, unpleasant, or neither pleasant nor unpleasant—arises dependent on eye-contact as it really is, one gets not attached to the eye, gets not attached to forms, gets not attached to eye-consciousness, gets not attached to eye-contact, and gets not attached even to that feeling that arises dependent on eye-contact.

And for him as he abides unattached, unfettered, uninfatuated, contemplating the peril (in eye etc.), the five aggregates of grasping go on to future diminution. That craving which makes for re-becoming, which is accompanied by delight and lust, finding delight here and there, decreases in him. His bodily disturbances cease, his mental disturbances cease; his bodily afflictions cease, his mental afflictions cease; his bodily distresses cease, his mental distresses cease; and he experiences physical and mental happiness. Whatever view such a one has, that becomes for him Right View; whatever intention he has, that becomes for him Right Intention; whatever effort he puts forth, that becomes for him Right Effort; whatever mindfulness he has, that becomes for him Right Mindfulness; and whatever concentration he has, that becomes for him Right Concentration. But his bodily actions and his verbal actions and his livelihood have already been purified earlier. So this Noble Eightfold Path comes to be perfected in him by development.

While this Noble Eightfold Path is being developed by him thus, the four foundations of mindfulness also go on to fulfilment through development and the four right efforts ... and the four bases of psychic power ... and the five spiritual faculties ... and the five powers ... and the seven factors of enlightenment go on to fulfilment through development. And in him these two things occur coupled together: serenity and insight. Those things that should be fully understood by direct knowledge—he fully understands by direct knowledge. These things that should be abandoned by direct knowledge—he abandons by direct knowledge. Those things that should be developed by direct knowledge— he develops by direct knowledge. And those things that should be realized by direct knowledge—he realizes by direct knowledge.

Mahāsaḷāyatanika Sutta, M.III,287ff.

APPENDIX 1

THE CALL TO THE MEDITATIVE LIFE

The intrinsic value of the life of a meditative monk is beyond estimation. There are various marvellous ways of life in this world. But there can hardly be a more marvellous way of life than that of a meditative monk. When you come to think about this, you have reason to congratulate yourself on taking up this way of life. This life of a meditative monk is not only invaluable, but pure and clean. All the other marvellous ways of life in this world are concerned with external things. They have to do with things external—with external mechanics. The life of a meditator, on the other hand, is concerned with the internal mechanics—the mechanics of mind-control. The Buddha was the greatest meditator of all times. The life of the meditative monk originated with him. The birth of a Buddha is an extremely rare phenomenon in the world. Not all who listen to his Dhamma take to this life of meditation; only a few of them take up the meditative life in earnest. Be happy that you are counted among these fortunate few.

Think about the tranquil results following from the practice of the tranquillizing Dhamma which the Buddha has preached. If, on some memorable day in your lives, you conceived the idea of renunciation—of going forth from home to homelessness—it was as the result of a powerful thought force within you. You should always recall that event as one of great significance in your lives. You were able to leave behind your father and mother, your wife and children, your relatives and friends, and your wealth, due to a powerful thought force and a spirit of renunciation aroused in you by listening to the Dhamma. You should not surrender this great will power under any circumstances. You may rest assured that the step you have taken is quite in keeping with the ideal type of going forth described in the discourses. The Sāmañña-phala Sutta (Discourse on the Fruits of Recluseship) of the Dīgha Nikāya portrays the true spirit of renunciation behind the act of going forth in these words:

> Now, a householder or a householder's son or someone born in some family or other listens to the Dhamma and on hearing the Dhamma, he conceives faith in the Perfect One. When he is possessed of that faith he reflects: "Full of hindrances is the household life—a path for the dust of passions. The 'going forth' is like being in the open air. It is not easy for one living the household life to live the holy life in all its fullness, in all its purity, with the spotless perfection of a polished conch-shell. Let me, then, cut off my hair and beard; let me clothe myself in saffron robes and let me go forth from home to homelessness." Then, before long, leaving behind his property, be it small or great, leaving behind his circle of relatives, be it small or great, he cuts off his hair and beard, he clothes himself in the saffron robes and goes forth from home to homelessness.
>
> Digha Nikāya I,62ff.

With this kind of going forth you have stepped into an environment most congenial to the development of the mind. But, as in any other adventure, here too one has to be on one's guard against possible dangers. There are four stages in the life of a meditative monk:

(1) the occasion of going forth from the household life;
(2) the preliminary stage in his meditative life when he starts taming his mind in solitude with the help of a meditation subject;
(3) the encountering of dangers in the course of meditation in solitude;
(4) the stage of enjoying the results of his meditation.

To illustrate these stages we may, first of all, compare the going forth of a meditator to the arriving in a clearing of a jungle after passing through a thorny thicket. The household life is, in fact, a thicket full of thorns. But even though one has arrived in a clearing in the jungle, one has yet to face dangers coming from wild beasts and reptiles. So the meditator, too, in the preliminary stage of his practice has to encounter many distracting thoughts which are as dangerous as those wild beasts and reptiles. But with perseverance he succeeds in overcoming these dangers. This is like reaching a valuable tract of land after passing the dangerous area. At this stage the meditator has scored a victory over distracting thoughts. Now the world, together with its gods, looks up to him as a man of great worth and starts paying homage to him, worshipfully. But then the meditator, complacent with his initial success, parades through this valuable tract of land and gets bogged down in a morass. For gain, fame and praise are comparable to a morass. Some meditators get bogged down in this morass neck-deep and are unable to step out from it. Others get stuck in it for a while but manage to scramble out. Yet others see its dangers well in time and avoid it altogether.

The life of a meditator, then, is one which is not only precious, but precipitous in that it requires a great deal of caution. I do hope that these observations will give you some food for thought so that you will continue with your meditative life with refreshed minds and renewed vigour.

This meditative life should be steered with great care and caution, avoiding the rugged cliffs of aberration. If that thought force which once proceeded in the right direction lapses into an aberration halfway through, it will lose its momentum. Therefore, you should build up a keener enthusiasm and re-charge that thought force, cutting off all possibilities of lapses.

APPENDIX 2

THE EIGHTEEN PRINCIPAL INSIGHTS (From the *Visuddhimagga, XX,90)*

1. The contemplation of impermanence (*aniccānupassanā*): abandons the perception of permanence.
2. The contemplation of suffering (*dukkhānupassanā*): abandons the perception of pleasure.
3. The contemplation of non-self (*anattānupassanā*): abandons the perception of self.
4. The contemplation of disenchantment (*nibbidānupassanā*): abandons delighting.
5. The contemplation of fading away (*virāgānupassanā*): abandons lust.
6. The contemplation of cessation (*nirodhānupassanā*): abandons originating.
7. The contemplation of relinquishment (*paṭinissaggānupassanā*): abandons grasping.
8. The contemplation of destruction (*khayānupassanā*): abandons the perception of compactness.
9. The contemplation of passing away (*vayānupassanā*): abandons the accumulation (of kamma).
10. The contemplation of change (*vipariṇāmānupassanā*): abandons the perception of stability.
11. The contemplation of the signless (*animittānupassanā*): abandons the sign.
12. The contemplation of the desireless(*appaṇihitānupassanā*): abandons desire.
13. The contemplation of voidness (*suññatānupassanā*): abandons adherence (to the notion of self).
14. The higher wisdom of insight into phenomena (*adhipaññāvipassanā*): abandons adherence due to grasping at a core.

15. Correct knowledge and vision (*yathābhūtañāṇadassana*): abandons adherence due to confusion.
16. The contemplation of danger (*ādīnavānupassanā*): abandons adherence due to attachment.
17. The contemplation of reflection (*paṭisankhānupassanā*): abandons non-reflection.
18. The contemplation of turning away (*vivaṭṭānupassanā*): abandons adherence due to bondage.

Characteristic of Impermanence: Nos. 1, 6, 8, 9, 10, 11, 14
Characteristic of Pain (Suffering): Nos. 2, 4, 5, 12, 16
Characteristic of Not-self: Nos. 3, 7, 13, 15, 17, 18

APPENDIX 3

THE COGNITIVE SERIES IN JHĀNA AND THE PATH

The cognitive series (*cittavīthi*) is an explanatory tool introduced in the Abhidhamma and the commentaries to account for the organization of acts of mind into purposive sequences. In the philosophy of mind underlying the Abhidhamma, the mental process falls into two general categories. One is passive consciousness, the other active consciousness. Passive consciousness consists of a succession of momentary mental states of a uniform nature, called the life-continuum (*bhavanga*). This type of consciousness runs through and beneath the whole existence of an individual from birth to death, interrupted only by the occasions of active consciousness. The life-continuum is a result of kamma generated in the past existence, and determines the basic disposition of the individual in the present. It is most prominent in deep sleep, even though it occurs undetected countless times each day during waking hours in the brief intervals between active consciousness.

Whereas the mind-moments of the life-continuum are all identical in nature and function, those of active consciousness are quite different from each other. With their distinct characters and modes, these mind-moments are welded by certain laws of interrelatedness into a functionally effective sequence called the cognitive series (*cittavīthi*, literally, avenue of mental acts). Cognitive processes themselves are of different kinds, the principal distinction being that between a sensory process and an internal reflective process. A full sensory process consists of seventeen mind-moments. In the first part of this series, the mind adverts to the impinging sense-object, cognizes it, receives the impression, examines it and determines its nature. Up to this point the process occurs quite automatically, but following the determinative act the mind responds to the sense-object according to its own volition. It is in this phase, consisting of seven mind-moments called *javanas*, that fresh kamma is generated. Following the phase of *javanas*, the mind registers the impression, then lapses back into the life-continuum (*bhavanga*).

In a complete reflective series of the usual kind, in which the object is a reflectively considered sense-impression, a mental image or an idea, the process is less diversified. After emerging from the continuum, the mind adverts to the object, then enters the *javana* phase where it forms a volitional response; finally it registers the object and lapses once more into the life-continuum.

Jhanic attainment and path attainment are both instances of the reflective cognitive series, but differ significantly from the usual kind of process. In the usual series the *javana* moments are all identical, but here they exhibit a progression of stages.

In the case of jhanic attainment, following the moment of adverting, the *javana* phase moves through five stages: preliminary work (*parikamma*); access (*upacāra*); conformity (*anuloma*); change-of-lineage (*gotrabhū*); full absorption (*appanā*). Some meditators start from the access stage itself without preliminary work. They are those whose spiritual faculties have already been well-prepared. Conformity is the application of the mind in accordance with the work already done, thus stabilizing one's gains. With change-of-lineage, the "lineage" in this context is the sense-desire sphere. This refers to the surpassing of the lineage of the sense- desire sphere and growing into (or developing) the "exalted lineage" (i.e. the fine-material and the immaterial spheres). The absorption stage is the jhāna itself, which can last from a single mind-moment to a long series of such moments, depending on the meditator's skill. The object of all the *javana* moments is the same, the counterpart sign (*paṭibhāganimitta*). We can depict the jhanic process as follows:

Lc	Md	Pw	Acc	Con	Chl	Abs
***	***	***	***	***	***	***

Lc — Life continuum
Md — Mind-door adverting
Pw — Preliminary work
Acc — Access
Con — Conformity
Chl — Change-of-lineage
Abs — Absorption

The three asterisks in each case indicate that each mind-moment has three sub-moments: arising, persisting and dissolution.

In the case of path-attainment, the preliminary stages are similar to those for jhāna, but here change-of-lineage involves surpassing the mundane plane to develop the supramundane. The culmination of the process is the path and fruit. The path invariably lasts only for one moment. The fruit lasts two moments when preliminary work is included, three moments when preliminary work is omitted. A full path-attainment can be depicted thus:

Lc	Md	Pw	Acc	Con	Chl	P	F	F	Lc
***	***	***	***	***	***	***	***	***	***

P — Path
F — Fruit

APPENDIX 4

ONENESS

It is said in the *Paṭisambhidāmagga*:

> The mind cleansed in these six respects becomes purified and reaches oneness. And what are these onenesses?
>
> (1) The oneness aroused by the recollection of liberality;
>
> (2) the oneness aroused by the occurrence of the sign of serenity meditation;
>
> (3) the oneness aroused by the occurrence of the characteristic of dissolution; and
>
> (4) the oneness aroused by the occurrence of cessation.
>
> The oneness brought about by the recollection of liberality applies to those who are of a generous disposition. The oneness aroused by the occurrence of the sign of serenity meditation is attainable by those who apply themselves to the development of the mind. The oneness aroused by the occurrence of the characteristic of dissolution is peculiar to those who develop insight meditation. The oneness aroused by the occurrence of cessation is an experience of the Noble Ones. (Ps.I,166 ff.).

The "oneness" referred to here is none other than *concentration*. In this context, however, it is reckoned as fourfold according to the way in which various individuals come by that concentration. Out of these four, the first type of concentration can be attained either by reflecting on a particular act of liberality one has recently performed, or by mentally dwelling on other charitable deeds lying to one's credit.

The second type of oneness is the concentration leading to the exalted meditations which are still on the mundane level. It is also called absorption concentration. This comprises the four jhānas (absorptions) pertaining to the fine-material realms and the four meditative attainments of the four immaterial realms.

The third type of oneness is the concentration arisen in the course of insight meditation by way of reflection on the nature of *sankhāras*, or formations. Even without attaining a concentration of mind by means of any serenity meditation as such, a meditator practising insight meditation directs his mind to a particular section of formations. Now, if he goes on reflecting with perseverance, he will reach this oneness—this concentration. Ultimately, even this concentration will gather the same degree of strength as absorption concentration. As the meditator equipped with this kind of concentration continues to reflect on the formations, insight knowledges will develop. And at whatever moment he attains the supramundane path, that path-consciousness comes to be reckoned as a *jhāna* in itself, since it has some affinity with the factors proper to *jhānas*, such as the first *jhāna*. What are known as transcendental meditations in Buddhism are these supramundane levels of concentration within reach of the pure insight meditator.

The fourth type of oneness mentioned above is the concentration which the Noble Ones achieve when they attain to the fruits of the noble path (see pp.61–62). It is called "the oneness aroused by the occurrence of cessation" because it has Nibbāna as its object. The Noble Ones who have attained to a path-consciousness such as that of the Stream-enterer are able to re-arouse its fruit and enjoy the bliss of Nibbāna again and again. This is the normal practice of Noble Ones who have attained to one of the four stages of realization.[1]

One thing worth mentioning in this connection is that if the meditators practising insight meditation have already obtained either an access concentration or an absorption concentration through some kind of serenity meditation, it will be comparatively easy for them to achieve the desired results. On the other hand, one who takes up the practice of pure insight meditation without any prior experience in concentration will have to put forth, from the very start, an unremitting endeavour until the desired results are attained. He should, in fact, give up all expectations for his body and life in an all-out struggle to reach the Supreme Goal.

1.*Sotāpanna* (Stream-enterer); *Sakadāgāmi* (Once-returner); *Anāgami* (Non-returner); *Arahant* (the Accomplished One).

ABOUT THE AUTHOR

The author of this treatise, the Venerable Matara Sri Ñāṇārāma Mahāthera, was born in the town of Matara in southern Sri Lanka in the year 1901. He received his initial ordination (*pabbajjā*) as a novice monk in 1917 and his higher ordination (*upasampadā*) in 1922. He underwent a traditional monastic training and in the course of his higher education in the temple gained proficiency in knowledge of the Dhamma and in the scriptural languages, Pali and Sanskrit. While still living in the temple he already evinced a keen interest in meditation; subsequently, beginning in 1945, he left the confines of temple life and took to the life of a forest monk, dwelling and meditating in forest monasteries and meditation centres. In 1951 his patronage was sought by the Sri Kalyāni Yogāshramīyā Saṁsthā, an organization of meditation centres founded by the Venerable K. Sri Jinavaṁsa Mahāthera. This organization, which counts well over fifty branch centres in Sri Lanka, conferred upon him the eminent position of *mahopādhyāya*, chief preceptor and teacher, a position he held up to his death.

When a group of Burmese meditation masters headed by the Venerable Mahasi Sayadaw visited Sri Lanka in 1958, the Venerable Ñāṇārāma undertook a course of intensive training in the Burmese system of insight (*vipassanā*) meditation under the guidance of the Venerable U Javana, a senior pupil of Mahasi Sayadaw. In recognition of his ability, the Burmese meditation masters imparted to him the complete training necessary to become a fully qualified meditation master (*kammaṭṭhānācariya*).

An opportunity to apply this training and skill towards the guidance of others came in 1967, when he was invited to become the resident meditation master of the newly opened Mitirigala Nissaraṇa Vanaya, an austere meditation monastery founded by Mr. Asoka Weeraratne (now Venerable Bhikkhu Dhammanisanthi). As the meditation master of Mitirigala Nissaraṇa Vanaya, the venerable author gave instructions in meditation to a wide circle of meditators, including monks from Western countries.

The Venerable Ñāṇārāma passed away in April 1992, in his 92nd year, after a brief illness.

In addition to the present work the venerable author has several other publications in Sinhala to his credit, among them *Samatha-vidarsanā Bhāvanā Mārgaya,* an exposition of the path of meditation and *Vidirashanā Parapura,* a work on instruction and practice in the lineage of insight meditation. He was also the inspiration for *The Seven Contemplations of Insight* (*Sapta Anupassanā*).

Available from BPS

The Seven Contemplations of Insight

Prepared under the guidence of

Venerable Mātara Sri Ñāṇārāma Mahāthera

The present book evolved out of series of discourses on the "eighteen principal insights" that the Venerable Mātara Sri Ñāṇārāma Mahāthera gave in 1981 to the meditating monks at his monastery, the Nissaraṇa Vanaya Hermitage, in Mitirigala, Sri Lanka. Prepared by a pupil of Ven. Ñāṇārāma under his personal guidance, this book offers the reader an in-depth study of the first seven insights, which form a distinct and self-sufficient system known as "the seven contemplations" (*satta anupassanā*). At once theoretically rigorous yet pragmatic and precise, the book weaves together extensive material from the Buddha's discourses and the commentaries with concrete guidelines to mental training. By giving us a vivid picture of how these seven contemplations are to be applied in the actual course of meditation practice, this work serves to fill a major gap in our understanding of Buddhist insight meditation.

184 pages Order No. BP 512S

THE BUDDHIST PUBLICATION SOCIETY

The BPS is an approved charity dedicated to making known the Teaching of the Buddha, which has a vital message for people of all creeds. Founded in 1958, the BPS has published a wide variety of books and booklets covering a great range of topics. Its publications include accurate annotated translations of the Buddha's discourses, standard reference works, as well as original contemporary expositions of Buddhist thought and practice. These works present Buddhism as it truly is—a dynamic force which has influenced receptive minds for the past 2500 years and is still as relevant today as it was when it first arose. A full list of our publications will be sent upon request. Write to:

The Hony. Secretary
BUDDHIST PUBLICATION SOCIETY
P.O. Box 61
54, Sangharaja Mawatha
Kandy • Sri Lanka
E–mail: bps@ids.lk
Website: http: //www.lanka.com/dhamma